CONTENTS

SKILL OF THE WEEK LESSON PLANS

Social Skill of the WEEK Curriculum

42 Weeks of Lesson Plans for K-6 Classrooms

Amy Riccio, LMSW, MS

Laura Sokolofsky, MEd, NCC, LPC

Beth McGraw, MSEd

Boys Town, Nebraska

Social Skill of the Week Curriculum

Text and Illustrations Copyright © 2024 by Father Flanagan's Boys' Home
ISBN: 979-8-88907-018-4

Published by Boys Town Press, 13603 Flanagan Blvd., Boys Town, Nebraska 68010

For a Boys Town Press catalog, call **1-800-282-6657**
or visit our website: **BoysTownPress.org**

Publisher's Cataloging-in-Publication Data

Names: Riccio, Amy, author. | Sokolofsky, Laura, author. | McGraw, Beth, author.

Title: Social skill of the week curriculum : 42 weeks of lesson plans for K-6 classrooms / Amy Riccio, Laura Sokolofsky, Beth McGraw.

Description: Boys Town, NE : Boys Town Press, [2024]

Identifiers: ISBN: 979-8-88907-018-4

Subjects: LCSH: Social learning--Study and teaching (Elementary) | Social skills--Study and teaching (Elementary) | Social intelligence--Study and teaching (Elementary) | Children with social disabilities--Study and teaching (Elementary) | Student growth (Academic achievement)-- Handbooks, manuals, etc. | Teachers of children with social disabilities--Handbooks, manuals, etc. | Educational counseling--Handbooks, manuals, etc. | LCGFT: Lesson plans. | Instructional and educational works. | BISAC: EDUCATION / Counseling / Academic Development. | EDUCATION / Special Education / Behavioral, Emotional & Social Disabilities. | EDUCATION / Behavioral Management. | EDUCATION / Educational Psychology.

Classification: LCC: LC192.4 .R53 2024 | DDC: 303.3/24--dc23

Printed in the United States
10 9 8 7 6 5 4 3 2 1

Boys Town Press is the publishing division of Boys Town, a national organization serving children and families.

Instructions to Download Posters

ACCESS:
https://www.boystownpress.org/book-downloads

ENTER:
Your first and last names
Email address
Code: 888907sswc0184
Check yes to receive emails to ensure your email link is received.

Introduction

Today's classrooms are dynamic environments filled with students who have divergent life experiences, histories, identities, and families.

These students bring with them social and life skills that are neither universal nor uniform. Expecting or assuming young students will know how to follow instructions, stay on task, work cooperatively, or manage their emotions is a risky proposition.

Many students will enter your classroom lacking the required social skills, or an adequate mastery of the skills, to be consistently successful in school. Some may possess a range of life skills but struggle to transfer or adapt them to the classroom. Others simply have had little formal instruction or guidance, relying on their own habits and devices to get their needs met. Unfortunately, these habits may not always conform to the standards of appropriate or acceptable classroom behavior.

The *Skill of the Week Curriculum* is designed to help you empower every student to be more successful, regardless of circumstance or environment. It is a universal intervention, meaning it can be beneficial for all students, helping them flourish in school, at home, and in the community. Through social skills instruction, you give students more behavioral choices – choices that are healthier and more productive for them and for you.

Teaching young people new ways of thinking, new ways of feeling good, and new ways of behaving can have a transformative effect in the classroom. Research shows that social skills instruction coupled with other classroom-management practices can decrease aggressive behavior and increase academic engagement. When students learn to use the skills included in this curriculum, they can become your partners in creating a more productive, collaborative, and cooperative learning environment.

All of this teaching enables you to foster stronger, healthier relationships with your students.

How to Use This Curriculum

This curriculum consists of forty-two weeks of lesson plans, some of which can be combined to accommodate your academic calendar. All of the skills are easily adaptable to reflect a student's specific abilities and cultural norms. In addition to the forty-two skills, there are extension skills that can be taught in conjunction with a primary skill. For example, the skill of **Asking for Permission** includes the extension skill **Making a Request (Asking a Favor)**, and the skill of **Disagreeing Appropriately** includes the extension skill **Resolving Conflicts**.

Extension skills give you the option of teaching two skills together, during the same week, or the extension skill can be taught separately. Depending on the needs of your students and learning environment, you can customize your instruction accordingly.

Planned Teaching

The lessons are written to support daily Planned Teaching. Planned Teaching is an instructional strategy which draws upon the best evidence-based instructional practices for behavior. You can use Planned Teaching to introduce and reinforce the skills, and prepare students for future situations where they will need to use specific skills or behaviors. Planned Teaching involves the following four elements:

- **Introducing the skill** and explaining why it is being taught or where it can be used.

- **Describing the appropriate behavior**, which includes naming the skill and providing specific, observable behavioral steps.

- **Giving student-centered reasons** for using the skill in order to develop internal motivation and increase cooperation.

- **Practicing** the skill, which allows students to demonstrate the skill correctly, develop fluency, and gain confidence. It also provides you with opportunities to guide successful implementation.

Target Audience

All of the lessons are designed for K-6 general education classrooms, but they can be adaptable up to the eighth grade by using more age-appropriate videos, activities, and reading materials. Or, by simply leading a class discussion (centered around the four-steps of Planned Teaching) and incorporating opportunities for students to demonstrate the skills correctly.

Time

Each daily lesson can be taught in five to fifteen minutes, depending on the activities chosen each day. When time is limited, a brief discussion that covers the fours steps of Planned Teaching can be used.

Skill Posters

For your convenience and classroom use, a skill poster is included in each lesson. The posters highlight the skill name, the behavioral steps (numbered in the sequence in which they are performed), and a visual illustration of what the skill looks like in practice. These downloadable skill posters include a black-and-white illustration which can be distributed to students to color or decorate. You can place posters in classrooms and throughout the school to remind students how to follow and use the skills.

Role-Plays and Activities

Role-play is an effective instructional tool for helping students, especially younger ones, practice a skill's behavioral steps in a safe, controlled environment. Several true-to-life role-play scenarios for each skill are included in the appendix. If any scenario is not age-appropriate or relevant for your classroom, you can modify it accordingly, decide not to use that role-play with your students, or have students come up with their own situations to role-play.

While role-plays can be excellent practice, not all students consider them to be enjoyable learning activities. Some students may view role-play as embarrassing or an excuse to act out. They may intentionally engage in antics that distract from the learning, or they simply won't participate. If this is a concern for you, most lessons also involve other activities, such as large- and small-group discussion, journaling exercises*, video learning, and reading, that you can use in conjunction with, or as a replacement for, role-play.

*Most lessons include a writing activity that involves Social and Emotional Learning (SEL) Journals. If your classroom does not use SEL Journals, have students complete the activity using digital notebooks, personal journals and diaries, or regular notepaper.

Schedule of Skills

Choose a Skill of the Week schedule that best meets the needs of your learning community. You can follow the order in which the lessons are listed in this manual, which begins with the more basic skills and then graduates to the more advanced skills. However, skills can be taught in any order.

You may want to consider starting with skills that help support positive relationships, along with skills that help you and other adults better teach and guide students. Such skills can include **Greeting Others**, **Introducing Yourself**, **Following Instructions**, and **Accepting "No" for an Answer**.

It also can be helpful to teach a few skills that give students more agency or a voice (**Asking for Help** and **Getting the Teacher's Attention**, for example). Some students may view certain skills as more "rules" or simply another way for adults to manage and control them, instead of as skills that empower students to navigate their day and their life more successfully.

All of the skills in the curriculum were chosen because they commonly need development in K-6 general education classrooms. Individual skill lessons can be shortened or expanded based on time and student needs. Also, any lesson can be repeated when additional practice is needed.

Rewards and Benefits

This curriculum provides an efficient and engaging way to teach essential social skills. As students acquire and use these skills, their

---

SUGGESTED PRIORITIES for a SKILL of the Week SCHEDULE:

- *Build positive relationships and a positive school community.*
- *Improve adult/student interactions.*
- *Strive for the empowerment of a child over compliance.*
- *Improve student/student interactions.*
- *Teach skills that support academic achievement.*

---

behaviors will shift in healthier, more positive directions. This behavioral shift, while good for students, is equally advantageous for you. One noticeable benefit: fewer disruptions equal more time for instruction.

Use these lessons to forge deeper connections with students, making it easier to work through and get past behavioral mistakes. This also can be an opportunity for you to enhance the existing learning environment by building up each student's capacity to give and show respect, feel emotionally secure, strive toward common goals, and achieve lasting success.

In addition to the skills included in this curriculum, more than 100 others (from the basic to the complex) can be found in Teaching Social Skills to Youth, Fourth Edition, *published by Boys Town Press and available at boystownpress.org.*

About the Authors

Amy Riccio, LMSW, MS, earned bachelor's and master's degrees in social work and a master's degree in administration. She is a master trainer for Sources of Strength and Trauma Sensitive Schools. Amy has more than three decades of experience working with individuals in a variety of settings, including residential treatment, self-contained classrooms, dropout prevention programs, and the unhoused.

Laura Sokolofsky, MEd, NCC, LPC, earned her National Board Certification in counseling and is a licensed professional counselor. Her professional career includes work as an elementary educator as well as an elementary and middle school counselor. She currently serves as a school-based mental health therapist.

Beth McGraw, MSEd, spent more than a decade working with students who had behavioral and emotional disabilities. She then served eighteen years as a principal for programs serving students with disabilities. Beth has extensive experience implementing the Boys Town Education Model®.

Suggested Literature to Reinforce Skill Lessons

You can enhance the lessons by reading storybooks that feature characters who find themselves in situations where they need to learn and use specific life skills to overcome challenges and be successful. Reading storybooks aloud with students is a wonderful way to engage them with the lessons, foster greater comprehension, and improve skill acquisition.

Here is a list of the storybooks referenced in the curriculum and the skills they teach. Most titles can be ordered from BoysTownPress.org or wherever books are sold.

Herman Jiggle, Say Hello! by Julia Cook
Greeting Others
Introducing Yourself
Talking with Others (Having a Conversation)
Contributing to a Discussion (Joining in a Conversation)

The Name Jar by Yangsook Choi
Introducing Yourself

Hello World! by Kelly Corrigan
Introducing Yourself

The WORST Day of My Life EVER! and *The WORST Day of My Life EVER! Activity Guide for Teachers* by Julia Cook
Following Instructions
Following Written Instructions
Listening to Others

But It's Not My Fault by Julia Cook
Accepting Consequences
Caring for the Property of Others

When Sophie's Sorry Wasn't Enough by Jeff Tucker
Accepting Consequences
Making an Apology
Accepting Apologies from Others

Quiet Please Owen McPhee! by Trudy Ludwig
Listening to Others

Marcos, Did You Hear Me? by Bryan Smith
Listening to Others

I Have a Little Problem, Said the Bear by Heinz Janisch
Listening to Others

Wordy Birdy by Tammi Sauer
Listening to Others

Freddie the Fly: Motormouth by Kimberly Delude
Listening to Others
Talking with Others (Having a Conversation)
Contributing to a Discussion (Joining in a Conversation)

Strega Nona by Tomie dePaola
Listening to Others

Decibella and Her 6-Inch Voice by Julia Cook
Using an Appropriate Voice Tone (or Level)

Remi In Overdrive by Ashley Bartley
Staying on Task
Switching from One Task to Another

I Just Want to Do It MY WAY! and *I Just Want to Do It MY WAY Activity Guide for Teachers* by Julia Cook
Accepting Help or Assistance
Ignoring Distractions
Asking for Help

Freddie the Fly: Bee on, Buzz off
by Kimberly Delude
Ignoring Distractions

Are You Working Hard or Hardly Working?
by Bryan Smith
Completing a Task

How Did You Miss That? by Bryan Smith
Analyzing Tasks to Be Completed

Galimoto by Karen Lynn Williams
Analyzing Tasks to Be Completed

But I Need Your Help Now! by Bryan Smith
Getting the Teacher's Attention
Getting Another Person's Attention
Asking for Help

What Were You Thinking? by Bryan Smith
Getting the Teacher's Attention

My Mouth Is a Volcano by Julia Cook
Interrupting Appropriately

Teamwork Isn't My Thing, and I Don't Like to Share!
and *Teamwork Isn't My Thing, and I Don't
Like to Share Activity Guide for Teachers*
by Julia Cook
Working with Others
Sharing Something/Taking Turns

It's My Way or the Highway and corresponding
activity (*You Get More Bees with Honey Than
You Do Vinegar!*) by Julia Cook
Getting Another Person's Attention

Everyone's Contributions Count by Bryan Smith
Working with Others

I Just Don't Like the Sound of NO! and *I Just Don't
Like the Sound of NO! Activity Guide for
Teachers* by Julia Cook
Accepting "No" for an Answer
Accepting Decisions of Authority

Get Off My Lawn! by Michael Garland
Asking for Permission
Making a Request (Asking a Favor)
Making an Apology

Sorry, I Forgot to Ask! and *Sorry, I Forgot to Ask!
Activity Guide for Teachers* by Julia Cook
Asking for Permission
Making a Request (Asking a Favor)
Making an Apology

*The Misadventures of Michael McMichaels:
The Borrowed Bracele*t by Tony Penn
Asking for Permission

Priscilla and the Perfect Storm and *Priscilla
and the Perfect Storm Activity Guide*
by Stephie McCumbee
Using Anger Control (Self-Control) Strategies

Freddie and Friends: Bugging Out
by Kimberly Delude
Using Anger Control (Self-Control) Strategies

Of Course It's a Big Deal! by Bryan Smith
Using Anger Control (Self-Control) Strategies

That's Wrong! by Bryan Smith
Disagreeing Appropriately
Resolving Conflicts

The Great Compromise by Julia Cook
Working with Others
Disagreeing Appropriately
Resolving Conflicts

Zach Apologizes by William Mulcahy
Making an Apology

Just Help! by Sonia Sotomayor
Offering Assistance or Help

Why Should I Help? by Claire Llewellyn
Offering Assistance or Help

Catch the Ball! by Bryan Smith
Offering Assistance or Help

Kindness Counts by Bryan Smith
Offering Assistance or Help

All about Sharing by Bryan Smith
Sharing Something/Taking Turns

Thanks for the Feedback… (I Think?) by Julia Cook
Accepting Criticism (Feedback)
Accepting Compliments

The Technology Tail by Julia Cook
Using Technology Appropriately (in School)

Zombie Phone Kids by Michael Garland
Using Technology Appropriately (in School)

Freddie the Fly: Truth or Care by Kimberly Delude
**Correcting Another Person (Giving
Criticism/Feedback)**

Joy! You Find What You Look For by Gina Prosch
Showing Appreciation

The Power of an Attitude of Gratitude by Kip
"Mr. J" Jones
Showing Appreciation

Be Honest and Tell the Truth by Cheri J. Meiners
Self-Reporting Your Own Behaviors
Communicating Honestly

Well, I Can Top That! by Julia Cook
Self-Reporting Your Own Behaviors
Communicating Honestly

Cheaters Never Prosper by Julia Cook
Self-Reporting Your Own Behaviors
Communicating Honestly

The "I" in Integrity by Julia Cook
Self-Reporting Your Own Behaviors
Communicating Honestly

Responsible ME! Teacher Activity Guide
by Julia Cook
Self-Reporting Your Own Behaviors
Communicating Honestly

Isaac the Instigator by Jeff Tucker
Self-Reporting Your Own Behaviors
Communicating Honestly

Practicing Patience by Jennifer Law
Waiting Your Turn

Awesome Dawson It's NOT Your Turn! by Julia Cook
Waiting Your Turn
Sharing Something/Taking Turns

I Can't Believe You Said That! and *I Can't Believe You Said That! Activity Guide for Teachers*
by Julia Cook
Choosing Appropriate Words
Using Appropriate Language
Correcting Another Person
    (Giving Criticism/Feedback)

Pause Power by Jennifer Law
Asking for Time to Cool Down

Awesome Dawson Has Big Emotions by Julia Cook
Asking for Time to Cool Down

My Day Is Ruined! by Bryan Smith
Asking for Time To Cool Down

What's the Problem? by Bryan Smith
Asking for Clarification
Using Structured Problem-Solving (SODAS)

My Name's Sammy, and I'm No Snitch
by Jeff Tucker
Reporting Other Youths' Behavior
    (Peer Reporting)

Diamond Rattle Loves to Tattle by Ashley Bartley
Reporting Other Youths' Behavior
    (Peer Reporting)

Respect and Take Care of Things
by Cheri J. Meiners
Caring for the Property of Others

Is There an App for That? and *Is There an App for That? Activity Guide* by Bryan Smith
Making Positive Self-Statements/
Interrupting or Changing Negative
or Harmful Thoughts

Parker Plum and the Rotten Egg Thoughts
by Billie Pavicic
Making Positive Self-Statements/
Interrupting or Changing Negative
or Harmful Thoughts

Molly and the Runaway Trolley by Ashley Bartley
Making Positive Self-Statements/
Interrupting or Changing Negative
or Harmful Thoughts

Diversity Is Key by Bryan Smith
Valuing Differences

The Judgmental Flower by Julia Cook
Valuing Differences

Chapter Book Options

For older students or those with advanced reading skills, you may choose to add chapter books into the curriculum. Suggested titles include:

Everyone's Talking by Cindi Dodd, MEd

The Misadventures of Michael McMichaels series
by Tony Penn

Navigating Friendships series by Jennifer Licate

The Adventures of Jeff & Reed by Jen Kennedy
and Wendy Falk

Greeting Others

SUGGESTED MATERIALS	■ *Herman Jiggle, Say Hello!* by Julia Cook
LESSON OBJECTIVES	■ Determine when it's appropriate to greet others and how to greet someone in a variety of situations. ■ Demonstrate the skill of **Greeting Others** to peers and various adults (family members, strangers, etc.). ■ Examine how the skill of **Greeting Others** can be used to start a conversation. ■ Determine if the person they are greeting is a friend, stranger, or caring adult. ■ Evaluate situations to see if the person acknowledges their greeting.
ESSENTIAL QUESTIONS	✔ *Is it necessary to greet someone in every social situation?* ✔ *How can you determine the best way to greet someone?* ✔ *What are some different ways to greet someone?* ✔ *What is your next step, after greeting someone?*
LESSON ACTIVITIES AND ASSESSMENTS	■ Role-play scenarios that allow students to practice the skills of **Greeting Others** and **Introducing Yourself** while using different tones of voice (happy, sad, loud, calm, respectful, etc.). ■ Instruct students to make an entry in their *SEL Journals* describing their use of both skills along with the specific words and actions they use when greeting others and introducing themselves. ■ Ask students to keep track of how many times a day they use the skill of **Greeting Others** and with whom (family, stranger, friend, etc.).

★ SKILL STEPS

Greeting Others
1. Look at the person.
2. Use a pleasant voice.
3. Say, "Hi" or "Hello."

→

REASONS

- *Creates good first impression.*
- *Makes others feel welcome.*
- *Shows respect for others.*

✦ RELATED SKILL:

Introducing Yourself

Greeting Others

MONDAY	■ Ask students questions to assess their background knowledge and prior experiences using the skill. ■ State the name of the skill, its behavioral steps, and reasons to use the skill. ■ Model or demonstrate the skill. ■ Ask students to practice greeting each other using all three steps of the skill. ■ Read *Herman Jiggle, Say Hello!* by Julia Cook. Discuss what lessons students learned from reading the story.
TUESDAY	■ Identify and discuss various social situations where it is important to greet others. ■ Review the steps of the skill as well as the reasons for using it. ■ Ask students if they would greet their grandmother the same way they would greet a friend. Compare and contrast a few more examples, such as greeting the cashier at the store versus greeting the basketball coach. ■ Discuss different situations and why it is important to use the skill of **Greeting Others**.
WEDNESDAY	■ Review the steps of the skill as well as the reasons for using it. ■ Group students into pairs and have them role-play three different greeting scenarios. *(See appendix for sample scenarios.)* ■ Discuss how greetings in the role-play scenarios looked and sounded different.
THURSDAY	■ Model the steps of the skill and provide reasons for using it. ■ Ask students to share their experiences using the skill over the past week. ■ Ask students to identify the potential reactions of others when they greet them. ✦ Extend the learning by introducing the skill of **Introducing Yourself** and its behavioral steps. Demonstrate what it might look like to use the skills together. Discuss why it is appropriate to introduce yourself after greeting someone you have never met before.
FRIDAY	■ Review both skills, their steps, and the reasons for using them. ■ Have students make an entry in their *SEL Journals*. Ask them to explain why **Greeting Others/Introducing Yourself** are useful skills, and to describe the specific words and actions they use when demonstrating each skill.

Greeting Others

1. Look at the person.

2. Use a pleasant voice.

3. Say, "Hi" or "Hello."

Introducing Yourself

SUGGESTED MATERIALS	■ *The Name Jar* by Yangsook Choi ■ *Hello World!* by Kelly Corrigan
LESSON OBJECTIVES	■ Recognize when a social situation requires a personal introduction. ■ Demonstrate the skill of **Introducing Yourself** in a variety of social situations. ■ Determine if the person they are introducing themselves to is a potential friend, caring adult, or new acquaintance. ■ Evaluate why it is important to introduce yourself in appropriate, respectful ways.
ESSENTIAL QUESTIONS	✔ *When is the best time to introduce yourself?* ✔ *What does the skill of* **Introducing Yourself** *look and sound like?* ✔ *What are different ways you can introduce yourself that will help make a good impression (fist bump, handshake, head nod, etc.)?* ✔ *Why is it important to introduce yourself after greeting someone you've never met?* ✔ *Who are the people you should introduce yourself to at school?*
LESSON ACTIVITIES AND ASSESSMENTS	■ Role-play scenarios that allow students to practice introducing themselves while using different tones of voice (happy, excited, loud, soft, calm, respectful, etc.). ■ Instruct students to write in their *SEL Journals* each skill name and its behavioral steps. Challenge students to introduce themselves to at least two people at school they don't know. Ask students to write about the experience in their *SEL Journals*. ■ Ask students to make a list of situations where it would be appropriate to introduce themselves.

★ SKILL STEPS

Introducing Yourself

1. Look at the person. Smile.
2. Use a pleasant voice.
3. Say, "Hi, my name is…."
4. Shake hands (when appropriate).
5. When you leave, say, "It was nice to meet you, [state the other person's name]."

→

REASONS

- *Makes others feel welcome.*
- *Helps other people remember you.*

✚ RELATED SKILL:

Greeting Others

Introducing Yourself

MONDAY	■ Ask students questions to assess their background knowledge and prior experiences using the skill. ■ State the name of the skill, its behavioral steps, and reasons to use the skill. ■ Model or demonstrate the skill. ■ Have students work in pairs and practice introducing themselves. ■ Read *The Name Jar* by Yangsook Choi. *(Story may be read over a few days when time is limited.)* Discuss what lessons students learned from the story.
TUESDAY	■ Review the steps of the skill as well as the reasons for using it. ■ Share your own experiences using the skill. ■ Discuss why each step is important and have students practice with a partner. ▶ Watch a video, such as *K12 Grade 2 – English: Introducing Yourself* (4:32): https://www.youtube.com/watch?app=desktop&v=dTaz4vnUk3s.

WEDNESDAY	■ Review the steps of the skill as well as the reasons for using it.
	■ Role-play different types of introductions. *(See appendix for sample scenarios.)*
	■ Discuss students' experiences using the following prompts:
	  • *Do you feel differently when you introduce yourself to someone you sort of know versus a stranger?*
	  • *Which skill steps were the hardest? Easiest?*

THURSDAY	■ Demonstrate the skills of **Greeting Others** and **Introducing Yourself** together. ■ Role-play various scenarios where students can practice both skills together. *(See appendix for sample scenarios.)* ■ Read *Hello World!* by Kelly Corrigan. Lead a discussion on lessons learned from the story.
FRIDAY	■ Review the steps of both skills, along with reasons for using them. ■ Instruct students to make an entry in their *SEL Journals*. Ask them to write the name and behavioral steps of both skills – **Introducing Yourself** and **Greeting Others**. Then have them write about two situations, one where they introduce themselves to someone they've never met, and one where they greet someone whom they've met twice before. Have students compare and contrast the two situations. Ask for volunteers to share their examples, if appropriate.

Introducing Yourself

1. Look at the person. Smile.

2. Use a pleasant voice.

3. Say, "Hi, my name is...."

4. Shake hands (when appropriate).

5. When you leave, say, "It was nice to meet you, [state the other person's name]."

Following Instructions/ Following Written Instructions

SUGGESTED MATERIALS	■ *The WORST Day of My Life EVER!* and *The WORST Day of My Life EVER! Activity Guide for Teachers* by Julia Cook
LESSON OBJECTIVES	■ Recognize situations when they will need to follow written and/or verbal instructions. ■ Determine why it is important to follow instructions the first time they are given. ■ Demonstrate the skills of **Following Instructions** and **Following Written Instructions** in school, at home, and in other environments. ■ Evaluate why following instructions, whether written or verbal, is essential for success in school and other settings.
ESSENTIAL QUESTIONS	✔ *Why is it important to follow written and/or verbal instructions?* ✔ *How do you follow verbal/written instructions?* ✔ *Who is most likely to give you verbal instructions?* ✔ *What type of situations require you to follow written instructions?*
LESSON ACTIVITIES AND ASSESSMENTS	■ Instruct students to write in their *SEL Journals* each skill name and its behavioral steps. Have them write a paragraph describing a situation when it was hard for them to follow written or verbal instructions, including why it was difficult and what happened. Ask for volunteers to share their examples, if appropriate. ■ Role-play scenarios that allow students to practice the skills.

★ SKILL STEPS

Following Instructions

1. Look at the person.
2. Say, "Okay."
3. Do what you've been asked right away.
4. Check back.

→

REASONS

- *When you finish things quickly, you may have more time for things you like to do.*
- *If you do it right away, you'll probably remember what to do.*
- *Shows you are taking responsibility.*

✚ SKILL EXTENSION:

Following Written Instructions

Following Instructions/Following Written Instructions

MONDAY

- Ask students questions to assess their background knowledge and prior experiences using the skill.
- State the name of the skill and identify the steps.
- Model or demonstrate the skill.
- Read *The WORST Day of My Life EVER!* by Julia Cook. Discuss what lessons students learned from the story.
- Assign additional activities to support skill development using *The WORST Day of My Life EVER! Activity Guide for Teachers* by Julia Cook.

TUESDAY

- Review the steps of each version of the skill (see skill posters) and reasons for using them.
- Identify situations at school and in the classroom when the skill of **Following Written Instructions** is necessary.
- Divide the class into small groups and practice the skills of **Following Instructions** and **Following Written Instructions** using the following role-play scenarios:
  - *Write down all your homework assignments. Rank them in order from longest to shortest, along with their due date.*
  - *Write your name in the upper left corner of your notepaper. Write today's date in the upper right corner (use our classroom procedure for heading a paper). In the center of the page, draw a picture of a place you would like to visit someday, your favorite food, or a favorite game.*
  - *Play the game "Simon Says."*

WEDNESDAY

- Review the steps of each version of the skill and the reasons for using them.
- Model or demonstrate each skill.
- Instruct students to write down at least two reasons why it is important to follow instructions in each of the following situations:
  - *Parent tells you to clean your room.*
  - *Teacher asks you to move to a different seat.*
  - *Friend asks you to help them with a chore.*
  - *Grandpa asks you to look up directions to a new store and read them to him while he's driving.*
  - *You want to bake cookies, and the recipe is on the back of the box.*
- Ask for volunteers to share their answers and discuss as a group.

THURSDAY

- Review the steps of each version of the skill and the reasons for using them.
- Model or demonstrate each skill.
- Use the think-pair-share technique. Have students partner up to discuss or role-play situations during the school day when they have to follow instructions.
- Ask for volunteers to share their examples.

Following Instructions/Following Written Instructions

FRIDAY	■ Review the steps of each version of the skill and the reasons for using them. ■ Write down instructions on how to clean and organize students' workstations. Then have students practice following verbal and written instructions by cleaning their workstations. ■ Instruct students to write in their *SEL Journals* each skill name and its behavioral steps. Have them write a paragraph describing a situation when it was hard for them to follow written or verbal instructions, including why it was difficult and what happened. Ask for volunteers to share their examples, if appropriate.

Following Instructions

1. Look at the person.

2. Say, "Okay."

3. Do what you've been asked right away.

4. Check back.

Following Written Instructions

1. Read the instructions provided completely and carefully.

2. Do what the instructions tell you, in the order they are written.

3. Avoid changing or skipping any steps.

4. If you have questions or need clarification, ask an adult.

Accepting Criticism (Feedback)

SUGGESTED MATERIALS	■ *Thanks for the Feedback... (I THINK?)* and *Thanks for the Feedback... (I THINK?) Activity Guide for Teachers* by Julia Cook
LESSON OBJECTIVES	■ Recognize how to use the skill of **Accepting Criticism (Feedback)** in a variety of situations and settings. ■ Determine what the skill of **Accepting Criticism (Feedback)** looks and sounds like in school and at home. ■ Demonstrate the skill of **Accepting Criticism (Feedback)** in the classroom. ■ Evaluate how accepting criticism/feedback can lead to more success in school and other settings.
ESSENTIAL QUESTIONS	✔ *Why is it important to accept criticism (feedback)?* ✔ *What are some appropriate ways you can accept criticism?* ✔ *Who are the people most likely to give you feedback or criticism?* ✔ *How can you accept criticism or a consequence without getting angry or defensive?*
LESSON ACTIVITIES AND ASSESSMENTS	■ Use role-play scenarios that allow students to practice the skill. ■ Lead students in discussions about how characters from their favorite books, movies, and TV shows deal with criticism. ■ Instruct students to write in their *SEL Journals* about how they feel when their friends, teachers, and family members give them feedback, a criticism, or a consequence.

★ SKILL STEPS

Accepting Criticism (Feedback)

1. Look at the person.
2. Say, "Okay."
3. Stay calm (avoid arguing, complaining, or shutting down).

→

REASONS

- *Not as likely to repeat errors.*
- *People are more apt to give feedback and want to help you.*
- *Learn from your mistakes.*

+ RELATED SKILL:

Accepting Help or Assistance

Accepting Criticism (Feedback)

MONDAY

- Ask students to share their definitions of feedback and/or criticism.
- State the skill name and its behavioral steps.
- Provide reasons why accepting criticism (feedback) is important. Model the skill.
- Read and discuss *Thanks for the Feedback... (I THINK?)* by Julia Cook.
- Assign additional activities to support skill development using the *Thanks for the Feedback... (I Think?) Activity Guide for Teachers* by Julia Cook.
- Have students practice the skill using one or more of the following role-play scenarios:
  - *You received homework feedback.*
  - *A coach corrects your form during practice.*
  - *A parent tells you to change because your clothes don't match.*

TUESDAY

- Review the steps of the skill as well as the reasons for using it.
- Model the skill correctly. For example, ask students to give you feedback on how you pronounce a difficult name or how you demonstrate a current dance move incorrectly.
- Review the steps of the skill and discuss different ways to stay calm when feedback is difficult to hear.
- Use the think-pair-share technique. Have students partner up to discuss the skill using the following prompt: *Why is it important to accept criticism?*

WEDNESDAY

- Review the steps of the skill as well as the reasons for using it.
- Have students practice accepting criticism (feedback) from a peer.
- Discuss how accepting criticism (feedback) can help students in the classroom, at school, and in their community.
- Ask for volunteers to demonstrate the skill for the class.

THURSDAY

- Review the steps of the skill as well as the reasons for using it.
- Have students practice the skill using the following role-play scenarios:
  - *A friend says you're having a bad hair day.*
  - *The bus driver tells you your voice is too loud.*
  - *A friend says you're playing the game wrong.*
  - *A teacher corrects your work.*
- Discuss how students felt when receiving criticism and how they stayed calm.
- ✚ Extend the learning by discussing how the skill relates to **Accepting Help or Assistance**.
- Demonstrate the skill steps for **Accepting Criticism (Feedback)** and **Accepting Help or Assistance**.

Accepting Criticism (Feedback)

FRIDAY	<ul><li>Review the steps of both skills, and the reasons for using them.</li><li>Invite students to practice accepting feedback or accepting help by creating their own role-play scenarios.</li><li>Instruct students to write in their *SEL Journals* about how they feel when accepting feedback from their friends, teachers, and family members. Also have them identify situations when it is okay for them to accept help from others.</li></ul>

Accepting Criticism (Feedback)

1. Look at the person.

2. Say, "Okay."

3. Stay calm (avoid arguing, complaining, or shutting down).

Accepting Help or Assistance

SUGGESTED MATERIALS	■ *I Just Want to Do It MY WAY!* and *I Just Want to Do It MY WAY! Activity Guide for Teachers* by Julia Cook
LESSON OBJECTIVES	■ Recognize when the skill of **Accepting Help or Assistance** is a valuable skill to know. ■ Determine what offers of help or assistance look and sound like in a variety of settings. ■ Demonstrate the skill of **Accepting Help or Assistance** in various settings. ■ Evaluate situations where additional help or assistance may not be needed.
ESSENTIAL QUESTIONS	✔ *Why is it important to know how to accept help or assistance?* ✔ *What are some ways that help may be offered?* ✔ *Who are the people most likely to offer you help or assistance?* ✔ *What is the best way for you to accept or decline assistance?*
LESSON ACTIVITIES AND ASSESSMENTS	■ Invite students to practice the skill using one or more of the following role-play scenarios: • *Someone offers to help you pick up a mess.* • *Someone extends their hand to help you up after you tripped.* • *Your teacher asks if you need any help on an assignment.* ■ Ask students to write a story about accepting help or assistance. ■ Instruct students to make an entry in their *SEL Journals* describing a time when they chose not to accept help or assistance from someone.

★ SKILL STEPS

Accepting Help or Assistance

1. Look at the person.
2. If help is needed, say, "Yes, thank you."
3. If help is not needed, politely say, "No, thank you."

→

REASONS

• *Shows maturity and helps build confidence.*
• *Shows you can be responsible for your own actions.*

✚ RELATED SKILL:

Accepting Criticism (Feedback)

Accepting Help or Assistance

MONDAY

- Have students share any experiences where they provided criticism and then offered assistance to help someone correct their mistakes.
- State the name of the skill, its behavioral steps, and reasons to use the skill.
- Read *I Just Want to Do It MY WAY!*, then assign additional activities to support skill development using the *I Just Want to Do It MY WAY! Activity Guide for Teachers* by Julia Cook.
- Model or demonstrate how to accept help after receiving feedback.
- Invite students to practice both skills using one or more of the following role-play scenarios:
  - *Your mom says your hair is messy, and your sibling offers to help you fix it.*
  - *Your teacher gives you feedback on your homework and asks if you want help correcting your mistakes.*
  - *Your coach tells you your batting stance is not correct and offers to show you the correct way.*

TUESDAY

- Review the steps of both skills, and the reasons for using them.
- Explain how the skills complement each other.
- Use the think-pair-share technique. Have students partner up to discuss or role-play a situation where they needed to accept help after receiving feedback.

WEDNESDAY

- Review the steps of the skill **Accepting Help or Assistance** as well as the reasons for using it.
- Review how the skill of **Accepting Criticism (Feedback)** relates to the skill of **Accepting Help or Assistance**.
- Discuss the best ways to accept and/or deny assistance. (Examples can include: "Yes, thank you," and "No thanks. I've got it.")
- Have students pair up and practice both skills.

THURSDAY

- Demonstrate the skill steps of **Accepting Criticism (Feedback)** and **Accepting Help or Assistance**, then review how the two skills complement each other.
- Invite students to practice both skills using one or more of the following role-play scenarios:
  - *You are given feedback about your drawing, and you know it wasn't your best effort. The art teacher offers you help, but you know what you did wrong and don't need help.*
  - *Your brother said the tag on your shirt is showing and offers to fix it.*
  - *Your mom notices you are making the bed incorrectly and offers to help you.*

Accepting Help or Assistance

FRIDAY	■ Review the steps of both skills, and the reasons for using them. ■ Ask students to make an entry in their *SEL Journals* describing a time when they chose not to accept help or assistance from someone, including how the situation turned out and if they were able to handle the situation independently or had to go back and ask for help. If appropriate, ask for volunteers to share with the group. ■ Engage students in discussions about how using both skills has helped them, or in what situations using the skills proved difficult. ■ Encourage students to think about how the skills might be used in a future job/career, hobby, or other area of interest.

Accepting Help or Assistance

1. Look at the person.

2. If help is needed, say, "Yes, thank you."

3. If help is not needed, politely say, "No, thank you."

BOYS TOWN®

Accepting Consequences

SUGGESTED MATERIALS	■ *But It's Not My Fault* by Julia Cook ■ *When Sophie's Sorry Wasn't Enough* by Jeff Tucker
LESSON OBJECTIVES	■ Recognize when to accept a consequence for their actions in a variety of situations and settings. ■ Determine what accepting a consequence looks and sounds like in school and at home. ■ Demonstrate the skill of **Accepting Consequences** in various settings. ■ Analyze situations where accepting a consequence is a valuable skill to know and use.
ESSENTIAL QUESTIONS	✔ *How can you accept a consequence you've earned?* ✔ *What are some of the ways you can demonstrate the skill of **Accepting Consequences**?* ✔ *Who at school can help you accept your consequences?* ✔ *What are some things you can do to stay calm when receiving a consequence?*
LESSON ACTIVITIES AND ASSESSMENTS	■ Use role-play scenarios (see appendix) that allow students to practice the skill. ■ Instruct students to write in their *SEL Journals* about how accepting negative consequences has helped them in school and at home.

★ SKILL STEPS

Accepting Consequences

1. Look at the person.
2. Say, "Okay."
3. Stay calm (avoid arguing or making excuses).
4. If given instructions or suggestions on how to correct the situation, follow them.

→

REASONS

- *Not as likely to repeat behaviors that earn negative consequences.*
- *Motivates you to meet expectations and make better choices.*
- *More likely to follow the rules.*

Accepting Consequences

MONDAY	■ State the name of the skill and its behavioral steps.
	■ Discuss how the skill of **Accepting Consequences** differs from accepting feedback.
	■ Read and discuss ***But It's Not My Fault*** by Julia Cook, including how the character Noodle earned consequences but instead of accepting them he blamed others.
	■ Have students practice the skill using one or more of the following role-play scenarios:
	    • *You are told to stay after class for ten minutes to receive extra help, which keeps you from recess.*
	    • *Your teacher tells you and your friend that you have been talking too much and then instructs you to move to a different seat.*
	    • *The gym teacher says you were not being safe, and you will need to sit out the rest of the activity.*

TUESDAY	■ Review the steps of the skill as well as the reasons for using it. ■ Discuss scenarios or situations where negative consequences may be earned. Examples can include arriving late for an appointment, cursing in school, forgetting or not finishing homework, etc. ■ Model or role-play the skill with a student and offer feedback on how it feels to accept consequences. ■ Invite students to practice the skill with a partner using a role-play scenario (see appendix).
WEDNESDAY	■ Name the skill, its behavioral steps, and the reasons for using the skill. ■ Identify the various individuals who might deliver negative consequences to students based on their actions. ■ Instruct students to write in their *SEL Journals* the name of the skill, its behavioral steps, and why they should accept consequences. ■ Invite students to practice the skill with a partner using a role-play scenario they create.
THURSDAY	■ Review the steps of the skill, and the reasons for using the skill. ■ Ask students to describe situations during the past week when they had to accept a consequence. ▶ Watch a video, such as *Consequences for Kids: Character Education* (2:25): https://www.youtube.com/watch?v=LLZZYf_mlOA. ■ Lead a group discussion using the following prompt: *What did you learn from watching the video?*

Accepting Consequences

FRIDAY	■ Review the steps of the skill, and the reasons for using the skill. ■ Read ***When Sophie's Sorry Wasn't Enough***, then discuss what the character Sophie did to demonstrate her willingness to accept the consequences of her behavior. Assign additional activities to support skill development: DOWNLOADABLE ACTIVITIES: ***When Sophie's Sorry Wasn't Enough*** by Jeff Tucker. ■ Engage students in discussions about how using the skill has helped them, or in what situations it was difficult. ■ Group students in pairs and have them brainstorm different situations in which they will need to accept consequences. Then have them practice the skill by role-playing one or more of the situations they brainstormed.

Accepting Consequences

1. Look at the person.

2. Say, "Okay."

3. Stay calm (avoid arguing or making excuses).

4. If given instructions or suggestions on how to correct the situation, follow them.

Listening to Others

SUGGESTED MATERIALS	■ *The WORST Day of My Life EVER!* and *The WORST Day of My Life EVER! Activity Guide for Teachers* by Julia Cook ■ *Quiet Please, Owen McPhee!* by Trudy Ludwig ■ *Marcos, Did You Hear Me?* and *Marcos, Did You Hear Me? Downloadable Activities* by Bryan Smith ■ *I have a Little Problem, Said the Bear* by Heinz Janisch ■ *Wordy Birdy* by Tammi Sauer ■ *Strega Nona* by Tomie dePaola ■ *Freddie the Fly: Motormouth* by Kimberly Delude
LESSON OBJECTIVES	■ Recognize how to use the skill of **Listening to Others**. ■ Determine why listening is an important part of a conversation. ■ Demonstrate the skill of **Listening to Others** in the classroom, at school, and in other environments. ■ Analyze situations where listening is necessary at home, in school, and in the community.
ESSENTIAL QUESTIONS	✔ *How can you effectively listen to someone who is speaking to you?* ✔ *What are some ways you can demonstrate the skill of **Listening to Others**?* ✔ *Who are some important people you should always listen to at school? At home? In the community?* ✔ *What does it mean to actively listen to others?*
LESSON ACTIVITIES AND ASSESSMENTS	■ Instruct students to write the skill steps in their *SEL Journals*, including reasons why it's important to listen when others are speaking to them. ■ Provide students with an opportunity to teach the skill to their peers from other classes or students from a lower grade.

★ SKILL STEPS

Listening to Others

1. Look at the person who is talking and remain quiet.
2. Wait until the person is finished talking before you speak.
3. Show that you heard the person by nodding your head, saying, "Okay," etc.

➜

REASONS

- *You're more likely to be clear on the expectations/directions and be more apt to get them right the first time.*
- *Shows others you are paying attention.*
- *You'll probably know what's going on.*
- *It's the polite thing to do when someone else is speaking.*
- *Shows respect for others.*

Listening to Others

MONDAY	■ Ask students to explain how they can tell when someone is listening to them or not. ■ Name the skill, its behavioral steps, and the reasons for using the skill. ■ Read *The WORST Day of My Life EVER!* by Julia Cook or *Quiet Please, Owen McPhee!* by Trudy Ludwig. Discuss what students learned from the story. ■ Assign additional activities to support skill development using *The WORST Day of My Life EVER! Activity Guide for Teachers* by Julia Cook. ■ Model or demonstrate the skill. ■ Have students practice the skill by doing one or more of the following activities: 　• *Role-play this situation: A teacher tells the class to complete three tasks before moving on to a new activity.* 　• *Share with students information about an upcoming class activity or school event, then ask them to repeat back to you as many details as they can.* 　• *Play "Simon Says."*
TUESDAY	■ Review the steps of the skill, and the reasons for using the skill. ■ Read *Marcos, Did You Hear Me?*, then assign additional activities to support skill development: DOWNLOADABLE ACTIVITIES: *Marcos, Did You Hear Me?* by Bryan Smith. ■ Discuss the importance of listening and how to listen in a variety of situations (when a parent is talking about the morning's carpool plan, when crossing a dimly lit street, when multiple people are talking to you at once, etc.). ■ Model or demonstrate the skill with a volunteer and share how it feels when someone actively listens to you. ■ Pair students up and have each student share how they got their name, their favorite food, and why they like it, etc. Each partner should listen carefully and then share the information they remember with the class.
WEDNESDAY	■ Review the steps of the skill as well as the reasons for using it. ■ Identify situations when it is difficult to listen to someone (other distractions, lack of interest, feeling tired, angry, sad, or excited, etc.). Then discuss strategies for dealing with those types of situations. ■ Share examples you've witnessed around school or in the classroom of students using the skill. ■ Divide the class into small discussion groups and give them the following prompt: *Discuss how you can show others you're paying attention and listening to them.*
THURSDAY	■ Review the steps of the skill as well as the reasons for using it. ■ Read *I have a Little Problem, Said the Bear* by Heinz Janisch. ■ Discuss the book and ask students to share what they learned from reading the story. ■ Additional reading options include: 　• *Wordy Birdy* by Tammi Sauer 　• *Freddie the Fly: Motormouth* by Kimberly Delude 　• *Strega Nona* by Tomie dePaola

Listening to Others

FRIDAY	■ Review the steps of the skill as well as the reasons for using it. ■ Instruct students to write the skill steps in their *SEL Journals* and why it's important to listen when others are speaking to them. ■ Lead a class discussion using the following prompt: *How has the skill of **Listening to Others** helped you this week?* ■ Extend the discussion with the following prompts: *What are some things we do that make it hard for others to listen to us? What are some things we can do to make it easier for people to listen to us?*

Listening to Others

1. Look at the person who is talking and remain quiet.

2. Wait until the person is finished talking before you speak.

3. Show that you heard the person by nodding your head, saying "Okay," etc.

BOYS TOWN.

Using an Appropriate Voice Tone (or Level)

SUGGESTED MATERIALS	■ *Decibella and Her 6-Inch Voice* by Julia Cook
LESSON OBJECTIVES	■ Recognize when to alter voice tones or levels in various situations and settings. ■ Determine why using an appropriate tone of voice is important. ■ Demonstrate the skill of **Using an Appropriate Voice Tone (or Level)** in the classroom, cafeteria, and hallway. ■ Analyze situations where other people may change their voice tone.
ESSENTIAL QUESTIONS	✔ *Can you recognize the voice tone or level you're using?* ✔ *How can you modify your voice tone to match other voices in the room?* ✔ *Whose voice tone should you match or be similar to when you're at school? At home? In public?* ✔ *How can changing your voice tone help ensure people hear what you are trying to say?*
LESSON ACTIVITIES AND ASSESSMENTS	■ Practice the skill using role-play scenarios that encourage students to change their voice tones and voice levels. ■ Instruct students to write the skill name, its behavioral steps, and the reasons for using the skill in their *SEL Journals*. Then have them write about their experiences using the skill, including the situations/settings where it is easier for them to use the skill, and the situations/settings where it is more difficult for them to use the skill. ■ Provide students with an opportunity to teach the skill to their peers from other classes or students from a lower grade.

★ SKILL STEPS

Using an Appropriate Voice Tone (or Level)

1. Listen to the level of the voices around you.
2. Change your voice level to match.
3. Watch and listen for visual or verbal cues and adjust your voice if needed.

→

REASONS

- *It keeps the conversation private.*
- *Others are more likely to listen.*
- *People around you can hear.*

Using an Appropriate Voice Tone (or Level)

MONDAY	■ Ask students questions to assess their background knowledge and prior experiences using the skill. Have them identify different voice levels.
	■ Name the skill, its behavioral steps, and reasons for using the skill.
	■ Read *Decibella and Her 6-Inch Voice* by Julia Cook. Discuss what lessons students learned from the story.
	■ Model or demonstrate the skill.
	■ Have students practice the skill by doing one or more of the following role-play scenarios:
	  • *In a quiet library, you are talking with your friend about a book.*
	  • *Your coach asks you a question in gym class.*
	  • *Your teacher is explaining a new project, and you have a question.*
	  • *You are presenting a report in front of class.*

TUESDAY	■ Review the steps of the skill as well as the reasons for using it. ■ Model the skill with a student and discuss how to listen to the voices around you. ▶ Watch a video, such as *Appropriate Voice Tone* (6:57): https://www.youtube.com/watch?v=CWnKbVneh6I. ■ Have students practice the skill with a partner.
WEDNESDAY	■ Review the steps of the skill as well as the reasons for using it. ■ Identify and discuss situations where it can be difficult to choose/modify your voice tone. ■ Instruct students to write in their *SEL Journals* the skill name, its behavioral steps, and the reasons for using the skill.

THURSDAY	■ Review the steps of the skill as well as the reasons for using it.
	▶ Watch one or more of the following videos:
	  • *I Know Voice Levels* (4:48)
	    https://youtu.be/EcinDlh82Ps?si=QQerPY6GScm95_jN
	  • *The Way You Say Your Words Matters* (1:52)
	    https://youtu.be/rdPPnaGDxrs?si=XtJb-yY9s96krs8e
	  • *Tone of Voice: What You Really Mean* (15:01)
	    https://youtu.be/hPQyHXc1ksA?si=Zfmt3IMtYh9dH4xS
	■ Lead a discussion on what students learned.
	■ Divide the class into small groups and have them practice the skill.

Using an Appropriate Voice Tone (or Level)

FRIDAY	<ul><li>Review the steps of the skill as well as the reasons for using it.</li><li>Ask students to write in their *SEL Journals* their experiences using the skill, including the situations/settings where it is easier for them to use the skill, and the situations/settings where it is more difficult for them to use the skill.</li><li>Use the think-pair-share technique. Have students partner up and discuss where and when they will need to use the skill of **Using an Appropriate Voice Tone (or Level)**.</li><li>Group students in pairs and have them practice saying "Okay" in different voice tones (eager, resigned, sarcastic, angry, neutral, annoyed, excited, etc.).</li></ul>

Using an Appropriate Voice Tone (or Level)

1. Listen to the level of the voices around you.

2. Change your voice to match.

3. Watch and listen for visual and verbal cues and adjust your voice as needed.

Staying on Task

SUGGESTED MATERIALS	■ *Fix It with Focus* and *Fix It with Focus Downloadable Activities* by Bryan Smith ■ *I Just Want to Do It My WAY!* and *I Just Want to Do It My WAY! Activity Guide for Teachers* by Julia Cook ■ *Remi in Overdrive* and *Remi in Overdrive Downloadable Activities* by Ashley Bartley
LESSON OBJECTIVES	■ Demonstrate the skill of **Staying on Task** in school, at home, and in other environments. ■ Discuss why it is important to focus and stay on task. ■ Determine what staying on task looks and sounds like in their classroom. ■ Analyze situations where it may be difficult to stay on task. ■ Evaluate how staying on task might apply to various jobs or areas of interest.
ESSENTIAL QUESTIONS	✔ *What does the skill of **Staying on Task** mean or look like?* ✔ *Why is it important to stay on task?* ✔ *What can you do to focus and maintain your attention on a task?* ✔ *When you stay on task, how do you expect others to respond? Are your expectations reasonable, or do they need adjusting?* ✔ *Who can help you stay on task?*
LESSON ACTIVITIES AND ASSESSMENTS	■ Role-play scenarios that allow students to practice the skill of **Staying on Task**. ■ Instruct students to make an entry in their *SEL Journals* describing how they stay on task. ■ Provide students with an opportunity to teach the skill to their peers from other classes or students from a lower grade.

★ SKILL STEPS

Staying on Task

1. Look at your task or assignment.
2. Think about the steps needed to complete the task.
3. Focus all of your attention on the task.
4. Ignore distractions and interruptions.
5. Work until you are finished or instructed to stop.

→

REASONS

- *Less likely to have homework.*
- *More likely to complete your assignment in class.*
- *Less likely to disturb others.*

+ RELATED SKILL:

Ignoring Distractions

Staying on Task

MONDAY	■ Ask students to identify situations or tasks that require concentration and focus.
	■ Name the skill, its behavioral steps, and the reasons for using the skill.
	▶ What a video, such as *Social Emotional Learning Skill 10 Ignoring Distractions* (2:44): https://youtu.be/tuOeukujWWY?si=p4FHWWnFJbawc-5D.
	■ Identify and discuss reasons for using the skill of **Staying on Task** in school, at home, and in other environments.
	■ Model or demonstrate the skill.
	■ Have students practice the skill using the following role-play scenarios:
	  • *You are taking a test when the principal knocks on the door and asks to speak to the teacher immediately.*
	  • *As the teacher is lecturing, a student begins talking and trying to start a conversation with another student.*
	  • *You're reading the assigned book chapter and one of your classmates keeps tapping her pencil on the desk while another student walks to the front of the room and starts talking to the teacher.*

TUESDAY	■ Review the steps of the skill as well as the reasons for using it. ■ Read *Remi in Overdrive*, then assign additional activities to support skill development: DOWNLOADABLE ACTIVITIES: *Remi in Overdrive* by Ashley Bartley. ■ Role-play the skill with a volunteer and provide feedback about how to stay on task.
WEDNESDAY	■ Read *Fix It with Focus*, then assign additional activities to support skill development: DOWNLOADABLE ACTIVITIES: *Fix It with Focus* by Bryan Smith. ■ Ask students to identify situations where it is difficult to stay on task at school. ✚ Extend the learning by introducing the skill of **Ignoring Distractions** and its behavioral steps. Explain how this skill complements **Staying on Task** and how both skills can be used in school, at home, and in the community.
THURSDAY	■ Review the steps of the skill **Staying on Task** and the steps of the skill **Ignoring Distractions**, as well as reasons for using them. ■ Read *I Just Want to Do It MY WAY!* by Julia Cook. Discuss what students learned from the story. ■ Assign additional activities to support skill development using the *I Just Want to Do It My WAY! Activity Guide for Teachers* by Julia Cook. ■ Ask students to share examples of how they have used both skills in school or at home. ■ Ask students to identify situations where it can be difficult for them to stay on task. ■ As a group, discuss those situations and then brainstorm ideas or strategies that can help students keep their focus or regain their focus if they get distracted.

Staying on Task

FRIDAY	■ Review the steps of both skills as well as the reasons for using them. ■ Discuss situations where students have used both skills during the school week. ■ Ask students to make an entry in their *SEL Journals* describing how they stay on task at school or in the classroom and what specific actions or words they use to help them stay on task. ■ Group students in pairs and have them brainstorm different strategies they can use to stay on task and ignore distractions in situations where they have struggled to do so in the past. Ask for volunteers to share their strategies with the class.

Staying on Task

1. Look at your task or assignment.

2. Think about the steps needed to complete the task.

3. Focus all of your attention on the task.

4. Ignore distractions and interruptions.

5. Work until you are finished or instructed to stop.

Ignoring Distractions

SUGGESTED MATERIALS	■ *I Just Want to Do It MY WAY!* and *I Just Want to Do It MY WAY! Activity Guide for Teachers* by Julia Cook ■ *Freddie the Fly: Bee On, Buzz Off* and *Freddie the Fly: Bee On, Buzz Off Downloadable Activities* by Kimberly Delude
LESSON OBJECTIVES	■ Recognize when to use the skill of **Ignoring Distractions**. ■ Determine why it is important to stay on task and ignore distractions. ■ Demonstrate the skill of **Ignoring Distractions** in school, at home, and in the community. ■ Analyze situations where it may be difficult to stay on task when there are distractions.
ESSENTIAL QUESTIONS	✔ When is it important to ignore distractions and stay on task? ✔ What are things you can do to resist the urge to respond or react to distractions? ✔ Who are the people who can help you ignore distractions at school and at home? ✔ When is it appropriate to ask for help when you want to stop a distraction?
LESSON ACTIVITIES AND ASSESSMENTS	■ Provide students with an opportunity to teach the skill to their peers from other classes or students from a lower grade. ■ Create additional role-play scenarios that are relevant to your students. ■ Ask students to write a story about ignoring distractions, staying focused, and completing tasks. ■ Instruct students to make an entry in their *SEL Journals* describing a situation where it was hard for them to stay focused and ignore distractions, and what they did to regain their focus and finish the task.

★ SKILL STEPS

Ignoring Distractions

1. Avoid looking at the person or thing distracting you.
2. Stay focused on your task or assignment.
3. Resist the urge to respond to distracting questions, teasing, or laughing.
4. If necessary, report the distraction to a nearby adult.

→

REASONS

- *Helps you stay focused.*
- *More likely to get your work done faster.*

+ RELATED SKILL:

Staying on Task

Weekly Activities
Ignoring Distractions

MONDAY	■ Ask students to identify common distractions.
	■ Name the skill, its behavioral steps, and the reasons for using the skill.
	■ Model or demonstrate the skill.
	■ Read *I Just Want to Do It MY WAY!* by Julia Cook. Lead a discussion about the story and the character RJ. Ask students to identify things RJ did to ignore distractions and stay on task.
	■ Assign additional activities to support skill development using the *I Just Want to Do It MY WAY! Activity Guide for Teachers* by Julia Cook.
	■ Have students practice the skill using the following role-play scenarios:
	  • *Your parents ask you to clean the basement now while your older sibling is in the basement playing video games.*
	  • *The teacher is explaining an assignment to the class while your friend is whispering to you about something that happened at lunch.*
	  • *You have five minutes to complete a quiz, and your classmate is laughing and looking out the window.*

TUESDAY	■ Review the steps of the skill as well as the reasons for using it. ■ Model or demonstrate the skill. ■ Read *Freddie the Fly: Bee On, Buzz Off* by Kimberly Delude, then lead a discussion about what lessons Freddie learned. ■ Have students practice the skill steps with a partner.
WEDNESDAY	■ Review the steps of the skill as well as the reasons for using it. ■ Ask for volunteers to share examples of when or where it was difficult for them to ignore distractions and stay on task. Ask students to identify other situations in school or at home where it can be difficult to stay on task and ignore distractions. Write their responses on the board. ■ Ask students to brainstorm strategies for dealing with those distractions and staying on task. ■ Invite students to practice the steps of the skill by completing class work or a task while you [teacher] engage in some of the distractions written on the board.
THURSDAY	■ Review the steps of the skill as well as the reasons for using it. ■ Ask students to share their experiences using the skill in school and at home. ■ Invite students to practice the skill in small groups using role-play scenarios they create. ■ Assign additional activities to support skill development: DOWNLOADABLE ACTIVITIES: *Freddie the Fly: Bee On, Buzz Off* by Kimberly Delude.

Ignoring Distractions

FRIDAY	<ul><li>Model or demonstrate the skill.</li><li>Lead a group discussion about the importance of using the skill.</li><li>Ask students to make an entry in their *SEL Journals* describing a situation where it was hard for them to stay focused and ignore distractions, and what they did to regain their focus and finish the task. Ask for volunteers to share with the group.</li></ul>

Ignoring Distractions

1. Avoid looking at the person or thing distracting you.

2. Stay focused on your task or assignment.

3. Resist the urge to respond to distracting questions, teasing, or laughing.

4. If necessary, report the distraction to a nearby adult.

Completing a Task

SUGGESTED MATERIALS	■ *Are You Working Hard or Hardly Working?* and *Are You Working Hard or Hardly Working? Downloadable Activities* by Bryan Smith
LESSON OBJECTIVES	■ Recognize when and how to complete tasks they start. ■ Explain why it is important to use the skill of **Completing a Task**. ■ Demonstrate completing tasks in school, at home, and in other environments. ■ Analyze situations where it may be difficult to complete a task once they have started it.
ESSENTIAL QUESTIONS	✔ *What is an effective way to complete a specific task?* ✔ *What can you do to make sure your task is completed on time?* ✔ *Who are the people to ask/check with to ensure you have completed a task correctly?* ✔ *What should you do if you cannot complete a task or need help finishing it?*
LESSON ACTIVITIES AND ASSESSMENTS	■ Provide students with an opportunity to teach the skill to their peers from other classes or students from a lower grade. ■ Instruct students to write in their *SEL Journals* the name of the skill, its steps, and at least three reasons why completing tasks is important at school and at home. ■ Use Blended Teaching to combine an academic task or lesson with social skill instruction, such as completing an assignment and organizing or cleaning their work stations. ■ Create additional role-play scenarios that are relevant to your students.

★ SKILL STEPS

Completing a Task

1. Listen carefully to instructions.
2. Gather the tools or materials you need.
3. Begin working quickly, carefully, and neatly.
4. Remain focused on the task until it is done.
5. Check your work to make sure you followed all instructions.
6. Check back if appropriate.

→

REASONS

- *Shows responsibility.*
- *Builds confidence.*
- *You will most likely feel proud for accomplishing something.*

+ RELATED SKILL:

Analyzing Tasks to Be Completed

Completing a Task

MONDAY	■ Ask students to identify the various tasks they have throughout their day.
	■ Name the skill, its behavioral steps, and the reasons for using it.
	■ Model or demonstrate the skill.
	■ Invite students to practice the skill in small groups using one or more of the following role-play scenarios:
	  • *You are asked to write down all the ingredients needed to make your favorite food dish.*
	  • *When you get home from school, you are expected to finish your homework, set the dinner table, and walk the dog.*
	  • *Your teacher asks you to return all the recess games and equipment to their designated spot.*

TUESDAY	■ Review the steps of the skill as well as the reasons for using it. ■ Model or demonstrate the skill. ■ Read *Are You Working Hard or Hardly Working?* by Bryan Smith. ■ Have students practice the skill with a partner. ■ Assign additional activities to support skill development: DOWNLOADABLE ACTIVITIES: *Are You Working Hard or Hardly Working?* by Bryan Smith.
WEDNESDAY	■ Review the steps of the skill as well as the reasons for using it. ■ Share examples you've witnessed around school of students using the skill. ■ Instruct students to write in their *SEL Journals* the name of the skill, its steps, and at least three reasons why completing tasks is important at school and at home. ■ Encourage students to practice the skill throughout the day.
THURSDAY	■ Review the steps of the skill as well as the reasons for using it. ■ Group students in pairs and invite them to practice the skill again by creating their own role-play scenarios. ✚ Extend the learning by introducing the skill of **Analyzing Tasks to Be Completed.** ■ Ask students to explain how the skills of **Completing a Task** and **Analyzing Tasks to Be Completed** are similar to each other. ■ Ask students to identify situations where it can be difficult for them to complete tasks. As a group, discuss those situations and then brainstorm ideas or strategies for dealing with those situations.
FRIDAY	■ Have students name the steps of each skill and discuss reasons for using both skills (if applicable). ■ Ask students to share examples of how they have used the skill of **Completing a Task** over the past week, both at school and in their community. ■ Lead a discussion about how using the skills of **Completing a Task** and **Analyzing Tasks to Be Completed** has helped them, or in what situations it was difficult.

Completing a Task

1. Listen carefully to instructions.

2. Gather the tools or materials you need.

3. Begin working quickly, carefully, and neatly.

4. Remain focused on the task until it is done.

5. Check your work to make sure you followed all instructions.

6. Check back if appropriate.

Analyzing Tasks to Be Completed

SUGGESTED MATERIALS	■ *Galimoto* by Karen Lynn Williams ■ "Get Organized" activity from *ZEST: Live IT! Activity Guide* by Tamara Zentic ■ *How Did You Miss That?* and *How Did You Miss That? Downloadable Activities* by Bryan Smith
LESSON OBJECTIVES	■ Recognize when and how to use the skill of **Analyzing Tasks to Be Completed**. ■ Determine why it is important to analyze tasks. ■ Demonstrate the skill of **Analyzing Tasks to Be Completed** in school, at home, and in other environments.
ESSENTIAL QUESTIONS	✔ *What does analyzing a task mean?* ✔ *When is it important to analyze a task before completing it?* ✔ *What are effective ways to make sure you understand the task or assignment?* ✔ *Why should you analyze tasks before trying to finish them?*
LESSON ACTIVITIES AND ASSESSMENTS	■ Provide students an opportunity to analyze various tasks in the classroom or around school that need to be completed (cleaning up after lunch, organizing books on a shelf, completing group projects, etc.). ■ Instruct students to write in their *SEL Journals* the skill name, its behavioral steps, and reasons why it's important to first analyze tasks or assignments.

★ SKILL STEPS

Analyzing Tasks to Be Completed

1. Make sure you understand the task or assignment.
2. Identify the steps needed to complete the task.
3. Determine what should be done first, second, third, etc.
4. Complete the steps in order.

→

REASONS

- *Easier to understand and complete the task.*
- *Helps increase success when completing the task.*
- *Less likely to make a mistake.*

+ RELATED SKILL:

Completing a Task

Analyzing Tasks to Be Completed

MONDAY	■ Ask students to identify what they think is the best way to begin analyzing a task or assignment that needs to be completed.
	■ State the name of the skill, its behavioral steps, and reasons to use the skill.
	■ Model or demonstrate the skill.
	■ Have students practice the skill by doing one or more of the following role-play scenarios:
	  • *You are assigned to create a nature scene in art class. You must display, paint, and sketch the scene as well as write a description and give an oral presentation.*
	  • *Mom asks you to make a salad for dinner and set the table.*

TUESDAY	■ Review the steps of the skill as well as the reasons for using it. ■ Model or demonstrate the skill steps. ■ Read *How Did You Miss That?*, then assign additional activities to support skill development: DOWNLOADABLE ACTIVITIES: *How Did You Miss That?* by Bryan Smith. ■ Have students practice the skill with a partner before an upcoming class assignment or task.
WEDNESDAY	■ Review the steps of the skill as well as the reasons for using it. ■ Model or demonstrate the skill by analyzing a task that needs to be completed in the classroom. ■ Ask students to write in their *SEL Journals* the name of the skill, its behavioral steps, and reasons why it's important to first analyze tasks or assignments. ■ Have students practice the skill with a partner using a role-play scenario (see appendix).
THURSDAY	■ Review the steps of the skill as well as the reasons for using it. ■ Ask students to identify situations in school or at home where it is important to analyze tasks or assignments. Discuss their answers. ■ Ask for volunteers to describe what happened when they successfully used the skill in school or at home, or situations where they did not use the skill. ■ Read *Galimoto* by Karen Lynn Williams. Discuss which behavioral steps in the skills of ***Analyzing Tasks to Be Completed*** and ***Completing a Task*** the character demonstrated in the story.

Analyzing Tasks to Be Completed

FRIDAY

- Model or demonstrate the skill.
- Discuss reasons why the skill of **Analyzing Tasks to Be Completed** can benefit students.
- Discuss how they can use this skill when doing schoolwork or chores.
- Discuss how using the skill has helped them, or in what situations it was difficult.
- Group students in pairs and have them brainstorm future situations where they will need to analyze tasks and assignments.
- Assign additional activities to support skill development: "Get Organized" from *ZEST: Live It! Activity Guide* by Tamara Zentic. *"Use this activity to show students the importance of being organized and how a lack of organization and order can decrease enthusiasm, waste energy, and lead to unnecessary frustration. Energy is wasted and frustration mounts when we spend valuable time searching for items we need. In this activity, students recognize the importance of organizing tasks/activities and how it relates to zest."*

Analyzing Tasks to Be Completed

1. Make sure you understand the task or assignment.

2. Identify the steps needed to complete the task.

3. Determine what should be done first, second, third, etc.

4. Complete the steps in order.

Getting the Teacher's Attention

SUGGESTED MATERIALS	■ *But I Need Your Help Now!* and *But I Need Your Help Now! Downloadable Activities* by Bryan Smith ■ *What Were You Thinking?* and *What Were You Thinking? Downloadable Activities* by Bryan Smith
LESSON OBJECTIVES	■ Recognize how to get a teacher's attention in a variety of situations. ■ Determine what the skill of **Getting the Teacher's Attention** looks and sounds like in the classroom. ■ Demonstrate the skill of **Getting the Teacher's Attention**. ■ Examine how getting the attention of a teacher, when done in an appropriate, respectful way, can help them succeed in school.
ESSENTIAL QUESTIONS	✔ *What does the skill of **Getting the Teacher's Attention** look and sound like?* ✔ *When and why do you need to get the teacher's attention?* ✔ *How can you get the teacher's attention appropriately?* ✔ *What can you do to make sure the teacher knows you need their attention?* ✔ *When you can't get the teacher's attention right away, what should you do?*
LESSON ACTIVITIES AND ASSESSMENTS	■ Provide students with an opportunity to teach the skill to their peers from other classes or students from a lower grade. ■ Ask students to make an entry in their *SEL Journals* describing their use of the skill and what specific words/behaviors they say/do when getting the teacher's attention. ■ Use the think-pair-share technique. Have students partner up to discuss or role-play how to get the teacher's attention using the following prompt: *How do you get the teacher's attention when the teacher is busy helping another student?*

★ SKILL STEPS

Getting the Teacher's Attention

1. Look at the teacher.
2. Raise your hand and stay calm.
3. Wait until the teacher looks at you or says your name.
4. Ask your question or share your information in a calm voice.

→

REASONS

- *You are more apt to be called upon quickly.*
- *Doesn't disturb others around you.*
- *Keeps classroom more orderly and everyone has a chance to be heard.*

+ RELATED SKILL:

Getting Another Person's Attention

Getting the Teacher's Attention

MONDAY	■ Have students identify situations where they need to get the teacher's attention during class. ■ State the name of the skill, its behavioral steps, and the reasons for using the skill. ■ Read *But I Need Your Help Now!* by Bryan Smith, then discuss what lessons students learned from the story. ■ Have students practice the skill by doing one or more of the following role-play scenarios: 　• *You have a question about a homework assignment.* 　• *You need materials to complete a group project.* 　• *The teacher asks for a volunteer, and you want to help.*
TUESDAY	■ Review the steps of the skill as well as the reasons for using it. ■ Model or demonstrate the skill. ▶ Watch a video, such as *Getting the Teacher's Attention by Mrs. Lower's Class* (3:59): https://www.youtube.com/watch?v=wbrUHLIyBXc. ■ Group students in pairs and have them brainstorm the best way to get the teacher's attention in different situations, then have them role-play the situations with their partners.
WEDNESDAY	■ Review the steps of the skill as well as the reasons for using it, then model the skill. ■ Assign additional activities to support skill development: DOWNLOADABLE ACTIVITIES: *But I Need Your Help Now!* by Bryan Smith. ■ Share examples you've witnessed around school and in your classroom of students using the skill. ■ Have students practice getting the teacher's attention at various times throughout the school day.
THURSDAY	■ Review the steps of the skill as well as the reasons for using it. ■ Read *What Were You Thinking?*, then assign additional activities to support skill development: DOWNLOADABLE ACTIVITIES: *What Were You Thinking?* by Bryan Smith. ✚ Extend the learning by introducing the skills of **Getting Another Person's Attention** and **Interrupting Appropriately**. Review their behavioral steps and discuss how all three skills relate. ■ Model or demonstrate the steps of each skill.

Getting the Teacher's Attention

FRIDAY	■ Model or demonstrate the skill of **Getting the Teacher's Attention**. ■ Ask students to make an entry in their *SEL Journals* describing their use of the skill and what specific words/behaviors they say/do when getting the teacher's attention. ■ Engage students in discussions about how using the skill has helped them, or in what situations it was difficult. ■ Encourage students to think about how the skill might be applied at home or in the community (getting the attention of a parent, a sibling, a grandparent, a store clerk, a lifeguard, etc.).

Getting the Teacher's Attention

1. Look at the teacher.

2. Raise your hand and stay calm.

3. Wait until the teacher looks at you or says your name.

4. Ask your question or share your information in a calm voice.

Getting Another Person's Attention

SUGGESTED MATERIALS	■ *But I Need Your Help Now!* and *But I Need Your Help Now! Downloadable Activities* by Bryan Smith ■ *It's My Way or the Highway* and *You Get More Bees with Honey Than You Do with Vinegar! Downloadable Activity* by Julia Cook
LESSON OBJECTIVES	■ Recognize when they need to get another person's attention. ■ Determine what the skill of **Getting Another Person's Attention** looks and sounds like in a classroom. ■ Determine why it is important to get someone's attention in a respectful, appropriate way. ■ Demonstrate the skill of **Getting Another Person's Attention** in school, at home, and in the community. ■ Analyze situations where it may be important to get another person's attention.
ESSENTIAL QUESTIONS	✔ *What is the best way to get another person's attention?* ✔ *How can you get another person's attention in an appropriate way in different settings?* ✔ *When is it important to get another person's attention?* ✔ *What are some words you can say that show manners and respect when trying to get someone's attention?* ✔ *When trying to get another person's attention, how do you expect them to react?*
LESSON ACTIVITIES AND ASSESSMENTS	■ Instruct students to write in their *SEL Journals* the name of the skill and its behavioral steps. Ask them to include a paragraph describing situations at home or in the community where getting another person's attention is important or necessary. ■ Provide students with an opportunity to teach the skill to students from a lower grade. ■ Use the think-pair-share technique. Group students in pairs and give them the following prompt: *If you want to get an adult's attention on the playground or in the office, what should you do? What should your voice tone sound like and your body language look like?*

★ SKILL STEPS

Getting Another Person's Attention

1. Wait until the other person is available.
2. Look at the other person.
3. Say, "Excuse me…."
4. Wait until the person acknowledges you, then say what you want to say.

→

REASONS

- *Shows respect for others.*
- *More apt to get attention quickly.*

+ RELATED SKILL:

Getting the Teacher's Attention

Getting Another Person's Attention

MONDAY	<ul><li>Ask students to identify situations where it is necessary to get another person's attention.</li><li>State the skill name, its behavioral steps, and reasons for using the skill.</li><li>▶ Watch a video, such as *Getting Another Person's Attention* (0:57): https://www.youtube.com/watch?v=XkQcMSdcOv8.</li><li>Model or demonstrate the skill.</li><li>Have students practice the skill by doing one or more of the following role-play scenarios:<ul><li>*There is a spill in the hallway, but the custodian is talking to another adult.*</li><li>*You came to the office to call your mom, but the secretary is on the phone.*</li><li>*You see a friend hurt on the playground and need to get the attention of the playground aides.*</li></ul></li></ul>
TUESDAY	<ul><li>Review the steps of the skill as well as the reasons for using it.</li><li>Model or demonstrate the skill.</li><li>Share examples you've witnessed in your school of students using the skill.</li><li>Read ***But I Need Your Help Now!***, then assign additional activities to support skill development: DOWNLOADABLE ACTIVITIES: ***But I Need Your Help Now!*** by Bryan Smith.</li><li>Have students practice the skill with a partner.</li></ul>
WEDNESDAY	<ul><li>Review the steps of the skill as well as the reasons for using it.</li><li>Model or demonstrate the skill.</li><li>Ask students to write in their *SEL Journals* the name of the skill, its behavioral steps, and a paragraph describing up to three situations at home or in the community where getting another person's attention is important or necessary. Ask for volunteers to share their examples with the class.</li><li>Encourage students to practice the skill throughout the day and at home.</li></ul>
THURSDAY	<ul><li>Review the steps of the skill as well as the reasons for using it.</li><li>Ask students to share examples of how they have used the skill at school or with other adults/peers.</li><li>Identify people, areas, and/or situations (store, restaurant, public event, etc.) where students might use the skill in their community.</li><li>Have students practice the skill again using role-play scenarios they create.</li></ul>

Getting Another Person's Attention

FRIDAY	■ Model or demonstrate the skill. ■ Ask students to share examples of how they have used the skill in the past week. ■ Lead a discussion about how using the skill has helped them, or in what situations it was difficult. Explain how the skill steps might look different in an emergency situation and provide examples of what is, and is not, an emergency. ■ Read *It's My Way or the Highway*, then assign additional activities to support skill development: DOWNLOADABLE ACTIVITY: *You Get More Bees with Honey Than You Do with Vinegar!* by Julia Cook.

Getting Another Person's Attention

1. Wait until the other person is available.

2. Look at the other person.

3. Say, "Excuse me...."

4. Wait until the person acknowledges you, then say what you want to say.

Asking for Help

SUGGESTED MATERIALS	■ *I Just Want to Do It MY WAY!* and *I Just Want to Do It MY WAY! Activity Guide for Teachers* by Julia Cook ■ *But I Need Your Help Now!* and *But I Need Your Help Now! Downloadable Activities* by Bryan Smith
LESSON OBJECTIVES	■ Recognize when to use the skill of **Asking for Help**. ■ Determine why and when it is important to appropriately ask someone for help. ■ Demonstrate the skill of **Asking for Help** in school, at home, and in the community. ■ Analyze situations where they need to ask for help.
ESSENTIAL QUESTIONS	✔ *What are effective ways to ask someone for help?* ✔ *What types of help or assistance might you need?* ✔ *Who is the best person to ask for help when you're at school?* ✔ *Who might you ask for help when you're at home?* ✔ *Who is the best person to ask for help or assistance when you're in a public place?*
LESSON ACTIVITIES AND ASSESSMENTS	■ Provide students with an opportunity to teach the skill to students from a lower grade. ■ Ask students to make an entry in their *SEL Journals* describing their use of the skill and whether or not they received the help they needed. Then have them describe two situations where they must ask for help, including the specific words they would say. ■ Use the think-pair-share technique. Have students partner up to discuss and role-play how to ask for help using the following prompt: *Who might you ask for help if you get separated from a parent at an amusement park?*

★ SKILL STEPS

Asking for Help

1. Look at the person.
2. Ask the person if they have time to help you (now or later).
3. Clearly describe the kind of help you need.
4. Thank the person for helping you.

REASONS

→

- *You are less likely to become frustrated.*
- *You will get the help you need.*
- *You are more likely to complete the task correctly.*

+ RELATED SKILL:

Interrupting Appropriately

Asking for Help

MONDAY	■ Ask students to identify situations where they may need to ask someone for help.
	■ State the name of the skill, its behavioral steps, and reasons for using the skill.
	■ Model or demonstrate the skill.
	■ Have students role-play the following scenarios *(see appendix for more scenarios):*
	  • *You do not understand an assignment.*
	  • *Your shoes keep coming untied.*
	  • *You can't find your class materials.*

TUESDAY	■ Review the steps of the skill as well as the reasons for using it. ■ Model or demonstrate the skill. ■ Read *I Just Want to Do It MY WAY!*, then assign additional activities to support skill development using the *I Just Want to Do It MY WAY! Activity Guide for Teachers* by Julia Cook. ■ Invite students to practice the skill with a partner using a role-play scenario they create.
WEDNESDAY	■ Review the steps of the skill as well as the reasons for using it. ■ Model or demonstrate the skill. ■ Create additional role-play scenarios that are relevant to your students. ■ Ask students to make an entry in their *SEL Journals* describing their use of the skill and whether or not they received the help they requested.
THURSDAY	■ Review the steps of the skill as well as the reasons for using it. ■ Read *But I Need Your Help Now!* by Bryan Smith. Then lead a group discussion by asking students what they learned from the story. Suggested prompts include: *When was it okay for Isaac to interrupt an adult to get their attention? Why is asking for help important?* ■ Assign additional activities to support skill development: DOWNLOADABLE ACTIVITIES: *But I Need Your Help Now!* by Bryan Smith.
FRIDAY	■ Model or demonstrate the skill. ■ Discuss how using the skill has helped students, or in what situations it was difficult. ■ Discuss situations where students used the skill during the school week. ■ Ask students to make an entry in their *SEL Journals* describing situations where they can ask for help, what specific words they can use when asking someone for help, and how the skill can benefit them.

Asking for Help

1. Look at the person.

2. Ask the person if they have time to help you (now or later).

3. Clearly describe the kind of help you need.

4. Thank the person for helping you.

Interrupting Appropriately

SUGGESTED MATERIALS	■ *My Mouth Is a Volcano* and *My Mouth Is a Volcano Activity and Idea Book* by Julia Cook ■ *Decibella and Her 6-Inch Voice* by Julia Cook
LESSON OBJECTIVES	■ Recognize when to interrupt appropriately. ■ Determine when and why it is important to interrupt appropriately. ■ Demonstrate the skill of **Interrupting Appropriately** in school, at home, and in the community. ■ Analyze situations where they need to interrupt a conversation. ■ Determine what the skill of **Interrupting Appropriately** looks and sounds like.
ESSENTIAL QUESTIONS	✔ *What is the most appropriate way to interrupt someone?* ✔ *Why is it important to know how to interrupt appropriately?* ✔ *What words and/or actions can you use to interrupt someone that are respectful and show manners?* ✔ *When or where might it be important to interrupt another person's conversation?*
LESSON ACTIVITIES AND ASSESSMENTS	■ Ask students to make an entry in their *SEL Journals* describing a time when they interrupted someone in an inappropriate way. Have them answer the following questions: *How did it turn out? What would you do differently if given a second chance?* ■ Provide students with an opportunity to teach the skill to students from a lower grade. ■ Use the think-pair-share technique. Have students partner up to discuss the following prompts: *If you want to interrupt two adults who are talking in the hallway, what should you do? What should your body language and voice tone look and sound like?*

★ SKILL STEPS

Interrupting Appropriately

1. If you must interrupt a person, stand where you can be seen.

2. Wait until the person acknowledges you or signals you to come back later.

3. Say, "Excuse me for interrupting, but…."

4. Share your request or information quickly.

5. Thank the person for their time.

→

REASONS

- *More likely to get what you want/ need faster.*
- *Shows respect to others.*

✚ RELATED SKILL:

Asking for Help

Interrupting Appropriately

MONDAY	■ Ask students to identify situations where they will need to use the skill in school and at home. ■ State the skill name, its behavioral steps, and reasons for using the skill. ■ Model or demonstrate the skill. ■ Read *My Mouth Is a Volcano* by Julia Cook. ■ Lead a class discussion by asking students what they learned from the story. Suggested prompts can include: *What did Louis learn? Why is this skill important?* ■ Assign additional activities to support skill development using the ***My Mouth Is a Volcano Activity and Idea Book*** by Julia Cook. ■ Have students practice the skill by doing one or more of the following role-play scenarios: 　• *You have an idea to share with a friend, but they are texting their parents.* 　• *Your art pencil keeps breaking. You need to ask the teacher for a new one, but the teacher is talking to another student.* 　• *Your friend got hurt during recess and needs an adult's help, but the adults are in a conversation.*
TUESDAY	■ Review the steps of the skill as well as the reasons for using it. ■ Model or demonstrate the skill. ■ Use the think-pair-share technique. Have students partner up to discuss or write down situations where it may be necessary to interrupt another person's conversation or someone who is busy working. ■ Instruct each pair to role-play the situations they discussed or wrote down. ■ Ask for volunteers to role-play for the class the situations they discussed or wrote down.
WEDNESDAY	■ Review the steps of the skill as well as the reasons for using it. ■ Model or demonstrate the skill. ■ Ask students to make an entry in their *SEL Journals* describing a time when they interrupted someone in an inappropriate way, how it turned out, and what they would do differently if given a second chance. ■ Engage students in discussions about how using the skill has helped them, or in what situations it was difficult.

Interrupting Appropriately

THURSDAY	<ul><li>Review the steps of the skill as well as the reasons for using it.</li><li>Read *Decibella and Her 6-Inch Voice* by Julia Cook. Lead a group discussion and ask students to identify or describe situations where it's appropriate to use each of the five volumes of voice when interrupting someone.</li><li>Ask for volunteers to demonstrate the steps of the skill **Interrupting Appropriately**.</li><li>Create additional role-play scenarios that are relevant to your students.</li><li>Provide reasons for using the skill and ask students to explain how it is similar to the skill of **Asking for Help**.</li></ul>
FRIDAY	<ul><li>Model or demonstrate the skills of **Interrupting Appropriately** and **Asking for Help**.</li><li>Ask students to share examples of how they have used both skills in the past week, including in school, at home, and with friends, family, and other adults.</li><li>Encourage students to think about how both skills might be used outside of school (when they are playing with their friends, at sports practice, or at the dinner table, etc.).</li></ul>

Interrupting Appropriately

1. If you must interrupt a person, stand where you can be seen.

2. Wait until the person acknowledges you or signals you to come back later.

3. Say, "Excuse me for interrupting, but...."

4. Share your request or information quickly.

5. Thank the person for their time.

BOYS TOWN®

Working with Others

SUGGESTED MATERIALS	■ *Teamwork Isn't My Thing, and I Don't Like to Share!* and *Teamwork Isn't My Thing, and I Don't Like to Share Activity Guide for Teachers* by Julia Cook ■ *Everyone's Contributions Count* and *Everyone's Contributions Count Downloadable Activities* by Bryan Smith ■ *The Great Compromise* by Julia Cook
LESSON OBJECTIVES	■ Recognize how to work with others in a variety of situations and settings. ■ Demonstrate the skill of **Working with Others** in school, at home, and in other environments. ■ Analyze community-based situations to identify where, when, and with whom the skill of **Working with Others** may be used. ■ Evaluate how the skill of **Working with Others** might apply to various jobs or areas of interest.
ESSENTIAL QUESTIONS	✔ *Why is it important to be able to work with others?* ✔ *What do you need to do to work with others successfully?* ✔ *How do you know when it is necessary to work with others rather than by yourself?* ✔ *What does working with others look and sound like?*
LESSON ACTIVITIES AND ASSESSMENTS	■ Use role-play scenarios (see appendix) that allow students to practice the skill. ■ Instruct students to write in their *SEL Journals* about how working with others has helped them in school and at home. ■ Provide students with an opportunity to teach the skill to their peers from other classes or students from a lower grade.

★ SKILL STEPS	REASONS
Asking for Help 1. Identify the tasks to be completed. 2. Assign parts of the task to each person. 3. Discuss ideas in a calm, quiet voice, and let everyone share their ideas. 4. Work on tasks until completed.	• *Builds relationships.* • *Fosters more creativity.* • *Improves problem-solving and decision-making skills.*

Working with Others

MONDAY

- Ask students questions to assess their background knowledge and prior experiences using the skill. Suggested questions can include: *Describe a situation where you had to work with others. What went well? What was hard about working with others?*
- State the name of the skill, its behavioral steps, and reasons to use the skill.
- Model or demonstrate the skill.
- Have students practice the skill by doing one or more of the following role-play scenarios:
  - *Your group must work as a team to put the jigsaw puzzle together.*
  - *Your group must rearrange the bookshelf so the titles on the top shelves are about animals, the middle shelves have titles about famous people or biographies, and the bottom shelves have all the remaining titles.*
  - *Your group must gather all the art supplies it needs and then work together to draw a picture of the school lunchroom. Color the picture in, cut it out, and display it on the wall.*

TUESDAY

- Review the steps of the skill as well as the reasons for using it.
- Read ***Teamwork Isn't My Thing, and I Don't Like to Share!*** by Julia Cook, then lead a class discussion using the following prompts: *What does RJ learn? Why is teamwork important when we work with others?*
- Share examples you've witnessed in your classroom of students using the skill.
- Identify a classroom or school project and ask students to work together to complete the project.

WEDNESDAY

- Review the steps of the skill as well as the reasons for using it.
- Share examples you've witnessed around school of students using the skill.
- Identify people, areas, and/or situations where students might use the skill at home or with other significant adults or peers (teammates, neighborhood friends, family members/caregivers, etc.).
- Instruct students to write in their *SEL Journals*. Have them describe a situation where they had to work with others to complete a task, including what went well and what was challenging. Ask for volunteers to share their stories with the class, if appropriate.

Working with Others

THURSDAY	■ Review the steps of the skill as well as the reasons for using it. ■ Ask students to share examples of how they have used the skill in their community or with other adults/peers. ■ Read *Everyone's Contributions Count* by Bryan Smith, then lead a class discussion using the following prompts: *What does Amelia learn? Why is it important to work with others?*
FRIDAY	■ Review the steps of the skill as well as the reasons for using it. ■ Read *The Great Compromise* by Julia Cook, then lead a class discussion using the following prompts: *What did Cora June learn? Is it a good thing to be flexible or open-minded when working with others?* ■ Instruct students to write or draw in their *SEL Journals* about a time when they worked with others to successfully complete a task, or a time when they worked with others but **did not** successfully complete a task. Have them identify the reasons why working with others was or was not successful. Ask for volunteers to share their experiences with the group, if appropriate. ■ Encourage students to think about how the skill can be used when playing with their friends, participating in sports, or doing a class project.

Working with Others

1. Identify the tasks to be completed.

2. Assign parts of the task to each person.

3. Discuss ideas in a calm, quiet voice, and let everyone share their ideas.

4. Work on tasks until completed.

Switching from One Task to Another

SUGGESTED MATERIALS	■ *Remi in Overdrive* and *Remi in Overdrive Downloadable Activities* by Ashley Bartley
LESSON OBJECTIVES	■ Recognize when it is appropriate to switch from one task to another. ■ Analyze why it is important to know how to switch tasks. ■ Determine what the skill of **Switching from One Task to Another** looks and sounds like in their classroom. ■ Demonstrate the skill of **Switching from One Task to Another** in the classroom, at school, and in other environments.
ESSENTIAL QUESTIONS	✔ *What are the best ways to switch from one task to another?* ✔ *When is it necessary to switch to a different task?* ✔ *What does switching from one task to another look like in the classroom? At school? At home?* ✔ *Who can you ask for help if you don't know how or when to switch tasks?*
LESSON ACTIVITIES AND ASSESSMENTS	■ Use the think-pair-share technique and have students partner up to discuss the following questions: *In what types of situations is it easy for you to switch tasks? In what types of situations is it harder for you to switch tasks? What makes it harder, and is there anything you can do to make switching tasks easier?* ■ Instruct students to make an entry in their *SEL Journals* describing their use of the skill and what was most difficult or challenging for them. ■ Provide students with an opportunity to teach the skill to their peers from other classes or students from a lower grade. ■ Lead a group discussion about the importance of being able to switch tasks during emergency situations. Ask students to identify examples of emergency situations at school which would require them to switch tasks.

★ SKILL STEPS		REASONS
Switching from One Task to Another 1. Be prepared for a change to occur. 2. Look or listen for a cue to change tasks. 3. Leave your current task immediately. 4. Shift your focus to the new task quickly. 5. Stay focused on the new task until finished or given different instructions.	→	• *Helps you stay organized and be ready for what's next.* • *Allows us to use our time wisely, so we can have extra time to do fun activities.*

Switching from One Task to Another

MONDAY	<ul><li>Ask students to identify situations where they will need to switch from one task to another.</li><li>State the name of the skill, its behavioral steps, and reasons to use the skill.</li><li>Model or demonstrate the skill.</li><li>Have students practice the skill by doing the following role-play scenarios:<ul><li>*You are playing a game with a friend when a classmate asks you to help them move several boxes.*</li><li>*Your time on the computer is over, and you need to return to your desk.*</li></ul></li></ul>
TUESDAY	<ul><li>Review the steps of the skill as well as the reasons for using it.</li><li>Model or demonstrate the skill.</li><li>Share examples you've witnessed in your classroom of students using the skill.</li><li>Identify people, areas, and/or situations where students might use the skill at school (playground, cafeteria, library/media center, health office, counseling office, with a substitute teacher, etc.).</li><li>Explain any behavioral steps or skills which may need to be altered or added for those people, areas, and/or situations.</li><li>Read *Remi in Overdrive*, then assign additional activities to support skill development: DOWNLOADABLE ACTIVITIES: *Remi in Overdrive* by Ashley Bartley.</li></ul>
WEDNESDAY	<ul><li>Review the steps of the skill as well as the reasons for using it.</li><li>Share examples you've witnessed around school of students using the skill.</li><li>Identify people, areas, and/or situations where students might use the skill at home or with other significant adults or peers (teammates, neighborhood friends, family members/caregivers, etc.).</li><li>Instruct students to write in their *SEL Journals* about a time when they had to stop one task and switch to another, what was difficult or challenging about switching tasks, and why they were or were not successful.</li><li>Encourage students to practice the skill independently at home or around school and report back on how they did.</li></ul>

Switching from One Task to Another

THURSDAY	■ Model or demonstrate the skill of **Switching from One Task to Another**, and label the steps as you do each one. ■ Share with students examples or situations where you needed (or were asked) to switch tasks. ■ Ask students to share examples of how they have used the skill at home and in school. ■ Invite students to practice the skill with a partner using the following role-play scenarios: • *The teacher instructs you to get out your history book and begin reading Chapter 5. When you finish reading the first paragraph, your teacher instructs you to stop reading, put the book away, get your art supplies out, and draw a picture.* • *As you work on homework, your parent asks you to stop and go help your sibling search for a missing book. After you find it, you're told to go back and finish your homework.*
FRIDAY	■ Review the steps of the skill as well as the reasons for using it. ■ Ask students to share examples of how they have used the skill during the past week. ■ Engage students in discussions about how using the skill has helped them, or in what situations it was difficult. ■ Encourage students to think about how the skill might be used in a future job/career, hobby, or other area of interest.

Switching from One Task to Another

1. Be prepared for a change to occur.

2. Look or listen for a cue to change tasks.

3. Leave your current task immediately.

4. Shift your focus to the new task quickly.

5. Stay focused on the new task until finished or given different instructions.

Accepting "No" for an Answer

SUGGESTED MATERIALS	■ *I Just Don't Like the Sound of NO!* and *I Just Don't Like the Sound of NO! Activity Guide for Teachers* by Julia Cook
LESSON OBJECTIVES	■ Recognize how to accept no in a variety of situations and settings. ■ Acknowledge that accepting no does not mean never. It could mean not right now. ■ Demonstrate the skill of **Accepting "No" for an Answer** in school, at home, and in other environments. ■ Explore prior knowledge of how to accept no within the school environment. ■ Analyze community-based situations to identify where, when, and with whom the skill may be used. ■ Evaluate how the skill of accepting no might apply to various jobs or areas of interest.
ESSENTIAL QUESTIONS	✔ *Is it okay to ask for what you need?* ✔ *What will you do if the answer is no, not yes?* ✔ *How can you ask in a respectful way?* ✔ *What are some words you can say to demonstrate manners and respect when asking for something?* ✔ *Who is the best person to ask?* ✔ *Is this the best time to ask, or can it wait until later?* ✔ *When you ask, how do you expect others to respond? Are your expectations reasonable, or do they need adjusting?*

★ SKILL STEPS

Accepting "No" for an Answer

1. Look at the person.
2. Say, "Okay."
3. Stay calm (avoid arguing or complaining).
4. If you disagree, ask later.

REASONS

- *When you can accept a 'No' answer appropriately, you have a much better chance of getting a 'Yes' answer in the future.*
- *Shows respect, makes others respect you more, and makes your relationships better.*

✛ SKILL EXTENSION:

Accepting Decisions of Authority

Accepting "No" for an Answer

<table>
<tr>
<td>

LESSON ACTIVITIES AND ASSESSMENTS

</td>
<td>

- Role-play scenarios (see appendix) that allow students to practice the skill while using different tones of voice (mad, loud, quiet, sad, calm, etc.).

- Use the think-pair-share technique and have students partner up to discuss or role-play the skill of **Accepting "No" for an Answer** using the following prompts: *If you are told no, what are you going to do next? What do your voice tone and body language sound and look like?*

- Instruct students to write in their *SEL Journals* about their use of the skill, including the strategies they use to stay calm when told no.

- Provide students an opportunity to teach the skill to their peers from other classes or students from a lower grade.

- Ask students to write about or draw a situation where they accepted a 'No' answer. Have them share with a partner or the group.

</td>
</tr>
</table>

Accepting "No" for an Answer

MONDAY

- Ask students questions to assess their background knowledge and prior experiences using the skill. Questions can include: *Have you ever been told no? If so, how did getting a 'No' answer make you feel? Did you accept the answer right away, or did you try to turn no into yes?*
- State the name of the skill, its behavioral steps, and reasons to use the skill.
- Model or demonstrate the skill.
- Have students practice the skill with a partner using the following role-play scenarios:
  - *You ask a classmate if you can sit by them at lunch and are told no.*
  - *You forget your homework and ask the teacher if you can turn it in late. The teacher says no.*

TUESDAY

- Review the steps of the skill as well as the reasons for using it.
- ▶ Watch a video, such as *Accepting "No" as an Answer* (3:19): https://www.youtube.com/watch?v=Tt0LTY_nVCk.
- Share examples you've witnessed in your classroom of students using the skill.
- Identify people, areas, and/or situations (playground, cafeteria, library/media center, health office, counseling office, with a substitute teacher, etc.) where students might use the skill at school.
- Explain any behavioral steps or skills which may need to be altered or added for those people, areas, and/or situations.
- Invite students to practice the skill with a partner using a role-play scenario they create or one you provide (see appendix).

WEDNESDAY

- Review the steps of the skill as well as the reasons for using it.
- Share examples you've witnessed around school of students using the skill.
- Identify people, areas, and/or situations where students might use the skill at home or with other significant adults or peers (teammates, neighborhood friends, family members/caregivers, etc.).
- Explain any behavioral steps or skills which may need to be altered or added for those people, areas, and/or situations.
- Read *I Just Don't Like the Sound of NO!* by Julia Cook, then lead a class discussion using the following prompts: *What does RJ learn? Why is it important to accept no for an answer?*

Accepting "No" for an Answer

THURSDAY

- Review the steps of the skill as well as the reasons for using it.
- Ask students to share examples of how they have used the skill at home or with other adults/peers.
- Identify people, areas, and/or situations (store, restaurant, public event, etc.) where students might use the skill in their community.
- ✚ Extend the learning by introducing the skill of **Accepting Decisions of Authority** and its behavioral steps. Explain how this skill complements the skill of **Accepting "No" for an Answer** and how both skills can be used in school, at home, and in the community.

Accepting Decisions of Authority skill steps:

1. Look at the person.
2. Listen carefully to the person's decision without interrupting.
3. Avoid arguing or becoming angry.
4. When you have the opportunity to speak, use a calm voice.
5. Acknowledge the decision by saying "Okay" or "I understand."
6. If appropriate, request a reason or disagree appropriately at a later time.

- Instruct students to write in their *SEL Journals*. Have them write down the specific words they will say the next time they are told 'No' and then describe the coping strategy they will use to help them stay calm.
- Invite students to practice both skills using the following role-play scenarios:
  - *The playground you want to play at is temporarily restricted for a community event. A security guard says you cannot play in the park while the event is going on.*
  - *You are told by the store clerk that you are not old enough to buy a certain item.*
  - *The restaurant waiter informs you the menu item you wanted is no longer available.*

FRIDAY

- Review the steps of both skills and how they complement each other.
- Ask students to share examples of how they have used either skill in their community.
- Assign additional activities to support skill development using the *I Just Don't Like the Sound of NO! Activity Guide for Teachers* by Julia Cook.
- Encourage students to think about how the skills might be used in a future job/career, hobby, or other area of interest.
- Ask for volunteers to role-play the following scenario: *During recess, Taylor asks to join in a game of kickball. The other players say no.*
- Pause the role-play and ask the following questions: *What are some possible reasons Taylor was told no? What should Taylor say or do in response to being told no? What can Taylor do instead of playing kickball?*
- Resume the role-play by having volunteers act out the students' answers.

Accepting "No" for an Answer

1. Look at the person.

2. Say, "Okay."

3. Stay calm (avoid arguing or complaining).

4. If you disagree, ask later.

Accepting Decisions of Authority

1. Look at the person.

2. Listen carefully to the person's decision without interrupting.

3. Avoid arguing or becoming angry.

4. When you have the opportunity to speak, use a calm voice.

5. Acknowledge the decision by saying "Okay" or "I understand."

6. If appropriate, request a reason or disagree appropriately at a later time.

Asking for Permission

SUGGESTED MATERIALS	■ *Get Off My Lawn!* and *Get Off My Lawn! Downloadable Activities* by Michael Garland ■ *Sorry, I Forgot to Ask!* and *Sorry, I Forgot to Ask! Activity Guide for Teachers* by Julia Cook ■ *The Misadventures of Michael McMichaels: The Borrowed Bracelet* by Tony Penn
LESSON OBJECTIVES	■ Recognize how to ask for permission in a variety of situations and settings. ■ Acknowledge that asking permission might result in a yes, no, or not right now answer. ■ Demonstrate the skill of **Asking for Permission** in school, at home, and in other environments. ■ Explore prior knowledge of asking permission within the school environment. ■ Analyze community-based situations to identify where, when, and with whom the skill of **Asking for Permission** may be used. ■ Evaluate how the skill of **Asking for Permission** might apply to various jobs or areas of interest.
ESSENTIAL QUESTIONS	✔ *Is it okay to ask for what you need?* ✔ *What will you do if the answer is no, not yes?* ✔ *How can you ask in a respectful way?* ✔ *What are some words you can say to demonstrate manners and respect when asking for something?* ✔ *Who is the best person to ask?* ✔ *Is this the best time to ask permission, or can it wait for later?* ✔ *When you ask permission, how do you expect others to respond? Are your expectations reasonable, or do they need adjusting?*

★ SKILL STEPS

Asking for Permission

1. Look at the person.
2. Use a pleasant voice.
3. Say, "May I please…?"
4. Accept the answer calmly.

REASONS

- *Shows others you understand boundaries.*
- *Helps you build stronger friendships.*

✚ SKILL EXTENSION:

Making a Request (Asking a Favor)

Asking for Permission

LESSON ACTIVITIES AND ASSESSMENTS	■ Role-play scenarios (see appendix) that allow students to practice the skill of **Asking for Permission** while using a variety of voice tones (mad, loud, quiet, sad, calm, etc.). ■ Use the think-pair-share technique and have students partner up to discuss or role-play the skill of **Asking for Permission** using the following prompts: *How are you going to ask for permission? What does your voice tone sound like? What does your body language look like?* ■ Instruct students to write in their *SEL Journals* about how they use the skill, including the specific words/behaviors they say/do when asking for permission. Then have them write a paragraph or draw a comic strip about a time when they didn't ask for permission in an appropriate way. ■ Provide students an opportunity to teach the skill to their peers from other classes or students from a lower grade. ■ Read *Get Off My Lawn!* and *Sorry, I Forgot to Ask!*, then lead a class discussion about what students learned from the stories.

Asking for Permission

MONDAY	■ Ask students questions to assess their background knowledge and prior experiences using the skill. Questions can include: *Have you ever had to ask permission? What activities do you need permission to do or require you to ask someone first? (Examples can include getting a snack, using someone's property/toy/clothes/supplies, touching someone, etc.).* ■ State the name of the skill, its behavioral steps, and reasons to use the skill. ■ Model or demonstrate the skill. ■ Have students practice the skill with a partner by using a role-play scenario they create or one you provide (see appendix).
TUESDAY	■ Review the steps of the skill as well as the reasons for using it. ▶ Watch a video, such as *Asking for Permission: Role-Play Conversation for Kids* (10:38): https://www.youtube.com/watch?v=FZBjuwqn4xo&list=PLii5rkhsE0LfAiRdCqhWO17bq-2LIWKVU&index=4. ■ Read *Get Off My Lawn!* by Michael Garland, then lead a class discussion using the following prompt: *How could the kids have avoided the messy situation if they had used the skill of* **Asking for Permission**? ■ Share examples you've witnessed in your classroom of students using the skill. ■ Identify people, areas, and/or situations where students might use the skill at school (playground, cafeteria, library/media center, health office, counseling office, with a substitute teacher, etc.). ■ Explain any behavioral steps or skills which may need to be altered or added for those people, areas, and/or situations. ■ Invite students to practice the skill with a partner using a role-play scenario they create or one you provide (see appendix).
WEDNESDAY	■ Review the steps of the skill as well as the reasons for using it. ■ Share examples you've witnessed around school of students using the skill. ▶ Read *Sorry, I Forgot to Ask!* by Julia Cook, or watch the read-aloud video (10:28): https://www.youtube.com/watch?v=4XRQ72WMNks. ■ Lead a class discussion about the story using the following prompts: *What does RJ learn? Why is asking permission important?* ■ Assign additional activities to support skill development using the *Sorry, I Forgot to Ask! Activity Guide for Teachers* by Julia Cook.

Asking for Permission

THURSDAY

- Review the steps of the skill as well as the reasons for using it.
- Ask students to share examples of how they have used the skill at home or with other adults/peers.
- Identify people, areas, and/or situations (store, restaurant, public event, etc.) where students might use the skill in their community.
- ✛ Extend the learning by introducing the skill of **Making a Request (Asking a Favor)** and its behavioral steps. Explain how this skill complements the skill of **Asking for Permission** and how both skills can be used in school, at home, and in the community.

  Making a Request (Asking a Favor) skill steps:
  1. Look at the person.
  2. Use a clear, pleasant voice.
  3. Express your request in the form of a question.
  4. If the person agrees, say, "Thank you."
  5. If they decline, accept "No" for an answer.

- Instruct students to write in their *SEL Journals*. Have them answer the following prompts:
  - *Why is it important to ask permission before you do or take something?*
  - *How would you feel if someone took something of yours without asking? If someone did do this, what would you do? What would you say?*
- Invite students to practice either skill with a partner using a role-play scenario they create or one you provide (see appendix).

FRIDAY

- Review the steps of both skills as well as the reasons for using them.
- Ask students to share examples of how they have used either skill in their community.
- Engage students in discussions about how the skill of **Asking for Permission** or the skill of **Making a Request (Asking a Favor)** has helped them, or in what situations it was difficult.
- Encourage students to think about how both skills might be used in a future job/career, hobby, or other area of interest.
- Assign the following reading: *The Misadventures of Michael McMichaels: The Borrowed Bracelet* by Tony Penn.
  - *Note: This is a chapter book which may be more suitable for older students (or younger students who have advanced reading skills).*

Asking for Permission

1. Look at the person.

2. Use a pleasant voice.

3. Say, "May I please…?"

4. Accept the answer calmly.

Making a Request (Asking a Favor)

1. Look at the person.

2. Use a clear, pleasant voice.

3. Express your request in the form of a question.

4. If the person agrees, say, "Thank you."

5. If they decline, accept "No" for an answer.

Using Anger Control (Self-Control) Strategies

SUGGESTED MATERIALS	■ *Priscilla and the Perfect Storm* and *Priscilla and the Perfect Storm Activity Guide* by Stephie McCumbee ■ *Freddie and Friends: Bugging Out* and *Freddie and Friends: Bugging Out Downloadable Activities* by Kimberly Delude ■ *Pause Power* and *Pause Power Downloadable Activities* by Jennifer Law ■ *Of Course It's a Big Deal!* and *Of Course It's a Big Deal! Downloadable Activities* by Bryan Smith
LESSON OBJECTIVES	■ Recognize how to use anger control strategies in a variety of situations and settings. ■ Demonstrate the skill of **Using Anger Control (Self-Control) Strategies** in a variety of school-related contexts, at home, or outside of school. ■ Explore prior knowledge of using anger control strategies within the school environment. ■ Analyze community-based situations to identify where, when, and with whom the skill of **Using Anger Control (Self-Control) Strategies** may be used. ■ Evaluate how using anger control strategies might apply to various jobs or areas of interest.
ESSENTIAL QUESTIONS	✔ *Is it okay to get angry?* ✔ *What will you do when you get angry?* ✔ *How can you use self-control strategies when you're angry?* ✔ *What are some words or phrases you can say to express your anger in a respectful way?* ✔ *What makes you angry?*

★ SKILL STEPS

Using Anger Control (Self-Control) Strategies

1. When someone or something makes you angry, pay attention to how your body is reacting.
2. Breathe slowly and deeply.
3. Instruct yourself to relax any tense muscles.
4. Ask for a few minutes alone to focus on calming down (if needed).
5. If calming down is difficult, ask a trusted person for help.

→

REASONS

- *Makes it less likely you will feel regret about your behavior.*
- *Shows maturity and you earn the respect of others.*
- *Helps you avoid damaging relationships and friendships.*

Using Anger Control (Self-Control) Strategies

LESSON ACTIVITIES AND ASSESSMENTS

- Read *Priscilla and the Perfect Storm*, then lead class discussions by asking students the following questions: *What does Priscilla learn? How can you take what Priscilla learned and use it to help you when you're angry?*
- Role-play scenarios (see appendix) that allow students to practice the skill of **Using Anger Control (Self-Control) Strategies** while using different tones of voice (mad, sad, loud, calm, respectful, etc.).
- Use the think-pair-share technique and have students partner up to discuss or role-play the skill of **Using Anger Control (Self-Control) Strategies** using the following prompt: *If you are told no, what are you going to do next?*
- Provide students an opportunity to teach the skill to their peers from other classes or students from a lower grade.
- Make a calm-down (stress) bottle using glitter. Shake the bottle and watch the glitter settle down.
- Lead a class discussion by asking students to identify situations that fit into each of the following Anger Levels. Use materials presented during the lesson (storybooks and videos) to help students brainstorm examples, such as someone takes your pencil, someone laughs at you, or rain ruins recess.
- Anger Levels:
    1. Low =
    2. Medium =
    3. High =
    4. Exploding =

Using Anger Control (Self-Control) Strategies

MONDAY	■ Ask students questions to assess their background knowledge and prior experiences using the skill. Suggested questions can include: *Have you ever been upset or angry? What are some things that make you upset or angry?* ■ State the name of the skill, its behavioral steps, and reasons to use the skill. ■ Model or demonstrate the skill. ■ Invite students to practice the skill independently or with others using a role-play scenario (see appendix). ■ Read *Pause Power*, then assign additional activities to support skill development: DOWNLOADABLE ACTIVITIES: *Pause Power* by Jennifer Law.
TUESDAY	■ Review the steps of the skill as well as the reasons for using it. ▶ Watch a video, such as *Why Do We Lose Control of Our Emotions* (6:47): https://www.youtube.com/watch?v=3bKuoH8CkFc. ■ Share examples you've witnessed in your classroom of students using the skill. ■ Invite students to practice the skill with a partner using a role-play scenario they create or one you provide (see appendix). ■ Identify people, areas, and/or situations where students might use the skill at school (playground, cafeteria, library/media center, health office, counseling office, with a substitute teacher, etc.). ■ Explain any behavioral steps or skills which may need to be altered or added for those people, areas, and/or situations.
WEDNESDAY	■ Review the steps of the skill as well as the reasons for using it. ■ Share examples you've witnessed around school of students using the skill. ■ Identify people, areas, and/or situations where students might use the skill at home or with other significant adults or peers (teammates, neighborhood friends, family members/caregivers, etc.). ■ Explain any behavioral steps or skills which may need to be altered or added for those people, areas, and/or situations. ■ Read *Priscilla and the Perfect Storm* by Stephie McCumbee, then lead a class discussion using the following prompt: *How does Priscilla manage her emotions in good ways and not-so-good ways?*

Using Anger Control (Self-Control) Strategies

THURSDAY

- Review the steps of the skill as well as the reasons for using it.
- Ask students to share examples of how they have used the skill at home or with other adults/peers.
- Identify people, areas, and/or situations (store, restaurant, public event, etc.) where students might use the skill in their community.
- Explain any behavioral steps or skills which may need to be altered or added for those people, areas, and/or situations.
- ▶ Watch a short film, such as *Just Breathe* by Julie Bayer Salzman and Josh Salzman (3:41): https://www.youtube.com/watch?v=RVA2N6tX2cg.
- Do a hands-on activity. Make a calm-down (stress) bottle using glitter. Shake the bottle and watch the glitter settle down.
- Use the think-pair-share technique. Have students partner up to discuss or role-play how to use anger control strategies using the following prompt: *What coping skill will you use to calm yourself down?*
- Read *Of Course It's a Big Deal!*, then assign additional activities to support skill development: DOWNLOADABLE ACTIVITY: *Of Course It's a Big Deal!* by Bryan Smith.

FRIDAY

- Review the steps of the skill as well as the reasons for using it.
- Ask students to share examples of how they have used the skill in their community.
- Read *Freddie and Friends: Bugging Out*, then assign additional activities to support skill development: DOWNLOADABLE ACTIVITY: *Freddie and Friends: Bugging Out* by Kimberly Delude.
- Engage students in discussions about how the skill of **Using Anger Control (Self-Control) Strategies** has helped them, or in what situations it was difficult.
- Encourage students to think about how the skill might be used in a future job/career, hobby, or other area of interest.

Using Anger Control (Self-Control) Strategies

1. When someone or something makes you angry, pay attention to how your body is reacting.

2. Breathe slowly and deeply.

3. Instruct yourself to relax any tense muscles.

4. Ask for a few minutes alone to focus on calming down (if needed).

5. If calming down is difficult, ask a trusted person for help.

Disagreeing Appropriately

SUGGESTED MATERIALS	■ *That's Wrong!* and *That's Wrong! Downloadable Activities* by Bryan Smith ■ *The Great Compromise* by Julia Cook
LESSON OBJECTIVES	■ Recognize how to disagree appropriately in a variety of situations and settings. ■ Demonstrate the skill of **Disagreeing Appropriately** in school, at home, and in other environments. ■ Explore prior knowledge of disagreeing appropriately within the school environment. ■ Analyze community-based situations to identify where, when, and with whom the skill of **Disagreeing Appropriately** may be used. ■ Evaluate how the skill of **Disagreeing Appropriately** might apply to various jobs or areas of interest.
ESSENTIAL QUESTIONS	✔ *Is it okay to disagree with someone?* ✔ *What words can you use to disagree respectfully?* ✔ *What can you do to prevent a disagreement from turning into a fight?* ✔ *When you disagree with others, how do you expect them to respond?* ✔ *When people treat each other disrespectfully, is it easier or harder to come to an agreement?* ✔ *How can you stay calm in a disagreement?*

★ SKILL STEPS

Disagreeing Appropriately

1. Look at the person.
2. Use a pleasant voice.
3. Say, "I understand how you feel" or "I hear what you are saying."
4. Respectfully tell why you feel differently.
5. Give a reason.
6. Listen to the other person.

→

REASONS

- *Keeps the disagreement from spiraling out of control.*
- *Prevents hurt feelings or making someone mad.*
- *Shows that you respect the other person.*

✚ SKILL EXTENSION:

Resolving Conflicts

Disagreeing Appropriately

LESSON ACTIVITIES AND ASSESSMENTS

- Read *That's Wrong!*, then lead class discussions by asking students the following questions: *What does Isaac learn? How can you take what Isaac learned and use it to help you when you have a disagreement with someone?*

- Role-play scenarios (see appendix) that allow students to practice the skill of **Disagreeing Appropriately** while using different tones of voice (mad, sad, loud, calm, respectful, etc.).

- Use the think-pair-share technique. Have students partner up and practice saying the word "Ok" using different voice tones, or attitudes, and then practice saying the word "Sorry" using different voice tones, or attitudes. Ask students the following question: *Can you hear how the meaning of the words can change depending on how the words are said?*

- Instruct students to write in their *SEL Journals* about how they can use the skill to resolve conflicts.

- Provide students an opportunity to teach the skill to their peers from other classes or students from a lower grade.

Disagreeing Appropriately

MONDAY

- Ask students questions to assess their background knowledge and prior experiences using the skill. Suggested questions can include: *Have you ever disagreed with someone? Has anyone ever disagreed with you? How did that make you feel?*
- State the name of the skill, its behavioral steps, and reasons to use the skill.
- Model or demonstrate the skill.
- Invite students to practice the skill independently or with others using a role-play scenario (see appendix).

TUESDAY

- Review the steps of the skill as well as the reasons for using it.
- ▶ Watch a video, such as *Disagreeing Respectfully* (6:18*):
  https://www.youtube.com/watch?v=dVIqIyjOl20.
  *Note: *The disagreeing respectfully lesson ends near the 6:18 mark, but the video continues with a musical number about empathy.*
- Lead a group discussion after watching the video using the following prompts: *What are examples of "blaming" words? How can you check your tone of voice? What tone is respectful? What tone is disrespectful?*
- Share examples you've witnessed in your classroom of students using the skill.
- Invite students to practice the skill with a partner using a role-play scenario they create or one you provide (see appendix).
- Identify people, areas, and/or situations where students might use the skill at school (playground, cafeteria, library/media center, health office, counseling office, with a substitute teacher, etc.).
- Explain any behavioral steps or skills which may need to be altered or added for those people, areas, and/or situations.

WEDNESDAY

- Review the steps of the skill as well as the reasons for using it.
- Share examples you've witnessed around school of students using the skill.
- Identify people, areas, and/or situations where students might use the skill at home or with other significant adults or peers (teammates, neighborhood friends, family members/caregivers, etc.).
- Explain any behavioral steps or skills which may need to be altered or added for those people, areas, and/or situations.
- ✚ Extend the learning by introducing the skill of **Resolving Conflicts** and its behavioral steps. Explain how this skill complements the skill of **Disagreeing Appropriately** and how both skills can be used in school, at home, and in the community.

Resolving Conflicts skill steps:
1. Take a deep breath and remain calm.
2. Listen to the other person's point of view.
3. Explain why you feel differently in a calm, clear voice and share your reasons.
4. Be flexible and willing to compromise.
5. Listen and discuss the situation until you find a solution.
6. If you are unable to reach an agreement, thank the person for trying to work with you.

Disagreeing Appropriately

WEDNESDAY	▶ Watch a video, such as *5 Ways to Respectfully Disagree – How to Disagree Politely* (3:22): https://www.youtube.com/watch?v=Y6EPw2FOEZA. ▶ Read ***That's Wrong!*** by Bryan Smith or ***The Great Compromise*** by Julia Cook. ■ Lead a class discussion about what students learned from the video and/or the stories.
THURSDAY	■ Review the steps of the skills as well as the reasons for using them. ■ Ask students to share examples of how they have used either skill at home or with other adults/peers. ■ Identify people, areas, and/or situations (store, restaurant, public event, etc.) where students might use the skills in their community. ■ Explain any behavioral steps or skills which may need to be altered or added for those people, areas, and/or situations. ■ Use the think-pair-share technique. Have students partner up and practice disagreeing appropriately and resolving conflicts. Use the following prompts to guide students: *stay calm, listen to each other's perspective, stick to the problem, think of solutions,* and *attack the problem NOT the person.*
FRIDAY	■ Review the steps of both skills as well as the reasons for using them. ■ Ask students to share examples of how they have used the skills in their community. ▶ Watch a video, such as *Kid President How to Disagree* (4:19): https://www.youtube.com/watch?v=dG5fkAgJmqc. ■ Engage students in discussions about how the skills of **Disagreeing Appropriately** and **Resolving Conflicts** helped them, or in what situations it was difficult. ■ Encourage students to think about how the skills might be used in a future job/career, hobby, or other area of interest.

Disagreeing Appropriately

1. Look at the person.

2. Use a pleasant voice.

3. Say, "I understand how you feel" or "I hear what you are saying."

4. Respectfully tell why you feel differently.

5. Give a reason.

6. Listen to the other person.

Resolving Conflicts

1. Take a deep breath and remain calm.

2. Listen to the other person's point of view.

3. Explain why you feel differently in a calm, clear voice and share your reasons.

4. Be flexible and willing to compromise.

5. Listen and discuss the situation until you find a solution.

6. If you are unable to reach an agreement, thank the person for trying to work with you.

Making an Apology

SUGGESTED MATERIALS	■ *When Sophie's Sorry Wasn't Enough* and *When Sophie's Sorry Wasn't Enough Downloadable Activities* by Jeff Tucker ■ *Sorry, I Forgot to Ask!* and *Sorry, I Forgot to Ask! Activity Guide for Teachers* by Julia Cook ■ *Get Off My Lawn!* and *Get Off My Lawn! Downloadable Activities* by Michael Garland ■ *Zack Apologizes* by William Mulcahy
LESSON OBJECTIVES	■ Recognize how to make an apology in a variety of situations and settings. ■ Demonstrate the skill of **Making an Apology** in school, at home, and in other environments. ■ Explore prior knowledge of making apologies within the school environment. ■ Analyze community-based situations to identify where, when, and with whom the skill of **Making an Apology** may be used. ■ Evaluate how the skill of **Making an Apology** might apply to various jobs or areas of interest.
ESSENTIAL QUESTIONS	✔ *How do you know when to make an apology?* ✔ *How do you make an apology?* ✔ *How can you stay calm when making an apology?* ✔ *What are some words you can say to express an apology in a sincere, respectful way?* ✔ *What does the word "apologize" mean?* ✔ *Have you ever apologized when you didn't want to or didn't mean it?* ✔ *Has anyone apologized to you in an insincere or phony way?*

★ SKILL STEPS

Making an Apology

1. Look at the person.
2. Use a serious and sincere voice.
3. Say, "I'm sorry for…" or "I want to apologize for…."
4. Explain how you plan to do better in the future.
5. If appropriate, offer to make restitution.
6. Thank the person for listening.

REASONS

- *Helps repair relationships and soothe hurt feelings.*
- *Makes forgiveness more likely.*
- *Shows respect.*

Making an Apology

LESSON ACTIVITIES AND ASSESSMENTS

- Role-play scenarios (see appendix) that allow students to practice the skill of **Making an Apology** while using different tones of voice (mad, sad, loud, calm, respectful, etc.).
- Use the think-pair-share technique. Have students partner up to discuss or role-play how to make an apology using the following prompts: *What does your voice tone sound like? What does your body language look like? If an apology is not accepted, what are you going to do next?*
- Instruct students to write or draw in their *SEL Journals* about a situation where they apologize, including the words they say and their body language. Then have them share their example with a partner.
- Provide students an opportunity to teach the skill to their peers from other classes or students from a lower grade.

Making an Apology

MONDAY	■ Ask students questions to assess their background knowledge and prior experiences using the skill. Suggested questions can include: *Have you ever apologized? Why did you apologize? How did it make you feel?* ■ State the name of the skill, its behavioral steps, and reasons to use the skill. ■ Model or demonstrate the skill. ■ Identify people, areas, and/or situations where students might use the skill at school (playground, cafeteria, library/media center, health office, counseling office, with a substitute teacher, etc.). ■ Have students practice the skill by identifying words and actions that are inappropriate or unhelpful when they make an apology. Then have them identify words and actions that are appropriate or helpful when making a sincere apology. ■ Invite students to practice the skill with a partner using a role-play scenario they create or one you provide (see appendix). ▶ Watch a video, such as *Social Skill Making an Apology* (2:58): https://www.youtube.com/watch?v=I3C5S-gMSaQ, or *Zack Apologizes* (6:17): https://www.youtube.com/watch?v=NvFWxNiLtZE.
TUESDAY	■ Review the steps of the skill as well as the reasons for using it. ■ Read ***Get Off My Lawn!*** by Michael Garland or ***Zach Apologizes*** by William Mulcahy, then lead a class discussion about what students learned from the story. ■ Share examples you've witnessed in your classroom of students using the skill. ■ Invite students to practice the skill with a partner using a role-play scenario they create or one you provide (see appendix). ■ Identify people, areas, and/or situations where students might use the skill at school (playground, cafeteria, library/media center, health office, counseling office, with a substitute teacher, etc.). ■ Explain any behavioral steps or skills which may need to be altered or added for those people, areas, and/or situations.
WEDNESDAY	■ Review the steps of the skill as well as the reasons for using it. ■ Share examples you've witnessed around school of students using the skill. ■ Identify people, areas, and/or situations where students might use the skill at home or with other significant adults or peers (teammates, neighborhood friends, family members/caregivers, etc.). ■ Explain any behavioral steps or skills which may need to be altered or added for those people, areas, and/or situations. ■ Instruct students to write an apology in their *SEL Journals* and then share their example with the person seated next to them (shoulder/elbow partner). If students read or watched the *Zach Apologizes* book or video, encourage them to follow the "four-square" apology process.

Making an Apology

THURSDAY	■ Review the steps of the skill as well as the reasons for using it. ■ Ask students to share examples of how they have used the skill at home or with other adults/peers. ■ Identify people, areas, and/or situations (store, restaurant, public event, etc.) where students might use the skill in their community. ■ Explain any behavioral steps or skills which may need to be altered or added for those people, areas, and/or situations. ▶ Reinforce the importance of accepting responsibility when making an apology. Read *When Sophie's Sorry Wasn't Enough* by Jeff Tucker, or watch a video, such as *Stop Making Excuses & Own Your Actions* (4:22): https://www.youtube.com/watch?v=RGJpO2qHUbQ. ■ Invite students to practice the skill with a partner using a role-play scenario they create or one you provide (see appendix).
FRIDAY	■ Review the steps of the skill as well as the reasons for using it. ■ Ask students to share examples of how they have used the skill in their community or with other adults/peers. ■ Engage students in discussions about how using the skill has helped them, or in what situations it was difficult. ■ Encourage students to think about how the skill might be used in a future job/career, hobby, or other area of interest. ■ Read *Sorry, I Forgot to Ask!*, then assign additional activities to support skill development using the ***Sorry, I Forgot to Ask! Activity Guide for Teachers*** by Julia Cook.

Making an Apology

1. Look at the person.

2. Use a serious and sincere voice.

3. Say, "I'm sorry for…" or "I want to apologize for…."

4. Explain how you plan to do better in the future.

5. If appropriate, offer to make restitution.

6. Thank the person for listening.

BOYS TOWN

Offering Assistance or Help

SUGGESTED MATERIALS	■ *Just Help!* by Sonia Sotomayor ■ *Why Should I Help?* by Claire Llewellyn ■ *Catch the Ball!* and *Catch the Ball! Downloadable Activities* by Bryan Smith ■ *Kindness Counts* by Bryan Smith
LESSON OBJECTIVES	■ Recognize how to use strategies to offer assistance or help in a variety of situations and settings. ■ Demonstrate the skill of **Offering Assistance or Help** in school, at home, and in other environments. ■ Explore prior knowledge of offering assistance or help within the school environment. ■ Analyze community-based situations to identify where, when, and with whom the skill of **Offering Assistance or Help** may be used. ■ Evaluate how the skill of **Offering Assistance or Help** might apply to various jobs or areas of interest.
ESSENTIAL QUESTIONS	✔ *How do you know when help will be needed?* ✔ *How can you respectfully ask if someone wants help?* ✔ *When someone offers you assistance, how do you want them to ask?* ✔ *How will you respond if someone tells you they don't want your help?* ✔ *How would you feel if someone was trying to help you, but you didn't want their help?*

★ SKILL STEPS

Offering Assistance or Help

1. Identify when help may be needed.
2. Ask the person if they need help.
3. Listen carefully to their response.
4. If the answer is yes, suggest how you can help and follow through.
5. If the answer is no, respect the answer.

→

REASONS

- *Others will see you as compassionate and caring.*
- *Strengthens your friendships.*
- *Makes you feel good.*

Offering Assistance or Help

LESSON ACTIVITIES AND ASSESSMENTS

- Role-play scenarios (see appendix) that allow students to practice the skill of **Offering Assistance or Help** while using different tones of voice (mad, sad, loud, calm, respectful, etc.).
- Use the think-pair-share technique. Have students partner up to discuss or role-play how to offer assistance and help using the following prompt: *When you offer assistance and help, how does that make our world better?*
- Provide students an opportunity to teach the skill to their peers from other classes or students from a lower grade.
- Use the Give One, Get One discussion strategy (sharing and seeking information with one another) and ask students the following questions:
  - *How can you offer help to someone else?*
  - *How can you help at home? At school? In your neighborhood?*
- Do a hands-on activity to introduce or reinforce the concept of empathy.
  1. Cut a sponge in the shape of a heart and partially fill a bowl with water.
  2. Pass around the dry, heart-shaped sponge so students can feel its weight. Explain to the class that the dry sponge represents our hearts when they are light and happy.
  3. Dip the sponge in the water (or ask for a volunteer to dip the sponge). Let students hold the wet, denser sponge over the bowl so they can feel how much heavier it is now.
  4. Tell students the heaviness represents a sad heart, and the heaviness people feel when they're sad. Point out how our words and actions can cause others to feel sad. Explain how the water dripping off the sponge represents tears, and we cry tears when we're sad. But tears also help move our sad feelings out of our hearts, making the hearts lighter again. You also can point out that humans are the only species that cries tears when they're sad.
  5. Wrap-up the activity by encouraging students to offer help and assistance when they notice someone's heart is heavy and dripping (tears). Remind them that when they have a heavy heart, they should ask for help or support.

Offering Assistance or Help

MONDAY

- Ask students questions to assess their background knowledge and prior experiences using the skill. Suggested questions can include: *Have you ever needed help? Have you ever helped somebody?*
- State the name of the skill, its behavioral steps, and reasons to use the skill.
- Model or demonstrate the skill.
- Identify people, areas, and/or situations where students might use the skill at school (playground, cafeteria, library/media center, health office, counseling office, with a substitute teacher, etc.).
- Have students practice the skill by identifying words and actions that are inappropriate or unhelpful when offering help. Then have them identify words and actions that are appropriate or helpful when offering assistance.
- Invite students to practice the skill with a partner using a role-play scenario they create or one you provide (see appendix).

TUESDAY

- Review the steps of the skill as well as the reasons for using it.
- Identify people, areas, and/or situations where students might use the skill at school (playground, cafeteria, library/media center, health office, counseling office, with a substitute teacher, etc.).
- Explain any behavioral steps or skills which may need to be altered or added for those people, areas, and/or situations.
- Share examples you've witnessed in your classroom of students using the skill.
- Read *Just Help!* by Sonia Sotomayor, or watch the *Just Help by Sonia Sotomayor Read Aloud* video (7:13): https://www.youtube.com/watch?v=5Pd-8-61Le4. Lead a class discussion about what the characters did to help others.
- Invite students to practice the skill with a partner using a role-play scenario they create or one you provide (see appendix).

WEDNESDAY

- Review the steps of the skill as well as the reasons for using it.
- Share examples you've witnessed around school of students using the skill.
- Identify people, areas, and/or situations where students might use the skill at home or with other significant adults or peers (teammates, neighborhood friends, family members/caregivers, etc.).
- Explain any behavioral steps or skills which may need to be altered or added for those people, areas, and/or situations.
- Use the think-pair-share technique. Have students partner up to discuss or role-play how to offer assistance or help using the following prompts: *Why should you help others? If you needed help, how would you ask for it?*
- Read *Why Should I Help?* by Claire Llewellyn, then lead a class discussion about what students learned from the story.

Offering Assistance or Help

THURSDAY	■ Review the steps of the skill as well as the reasons for using it.
	■ Ask students to share examples of how they have used the skill at home or with other adults/peers.
	■ Identify people, areas, and/or situations (store, restaurant, public event, etc.) where students might use the skill in their community.
	■ Explain any behavioral steps or skills which may need to be altered or added for those people, areas, and/or situations.
	■ Ask students to look for and identify examples of offering assistance, helping, and being kind in a book, such as *Kindness Counts* by Bryan Smith, or a video, such as *Kindness Boomerang – One Day* (5:44): https://www.youtube.com/watch?v=nwAYpLVyeFU.
	■ Have students practice the skill with a partner using the following role-play scenarios:
	   • *You see someone struggling to reach an item on a store shelf.*
	   • *While dining out, a member of the waitstaff spills a drink on your table.*

FRIDAY	■ Review the steps of the skill as well as the reasons for using it. ■ Ask students to share examples of how they have used the skill in their community or with other adults/peers. ■ Read *Catch the Ball!*, then assign additional activities to support skill development: DOWNLOADABLE ACTIVITIES: *Catch the Ball!* by Bryan Smith. ■ Engage students in discussions about how using the skill has helped them, or in what situations it was difficult. ■ Encourage students to think about how the skill might be used in a future job/career, hobby, or other area of interest.

Offering Assistance or Help

1. Identify when help may
be needed.

2. Ask the person if they need help.

3. Listen carefully to their response.

4. If the answer is yes, suggest how
you can help and follow through.

5. If the answer is no, respect
the answer.

Sharing Something/Taking Turns

SUGGESTED MATERIALS	■ *Teamwork Isn't My Thing, and I Don't Like to Share!* and *Teamwork Isn't My Thing, and I Don't Like to Share! Activity Guide for Teachers* by Julia Cook ■ *All about Sharing* and *All about Sharing Downloadable Activities* by Bryan Smith ■ *Awesome Dawson It's NOT Your Turn!* by Julia Cook
LESSON OBJECTIVES	■ Recognize when sharing/taking turns is appropriate in a variety of situations and settings. ■ Determine what sharing/taking turns look and sound like in their classroom. ■ Demonstrate the skill of **Sharing Something** in school, at home, and in other environments. ■ Examine how the skill of **Sharing Something** might be used with adults/peers outside of a school setting. ■ Analyze community-based situations to identify where, when, and with whom the skill of **Sharing Something** may be used. ■ Evaluate how the skill of **Sharing Something** might apply to various careers or areas of interest.
ESSENTIAL QUESTIONS	✔ *What does sharing something mean, and what does it sound and look like?* ✔ *What does it mean to make a trade?* ✔ *How can you take turns?* ✔ *What are some words you can say that show manners and respect when you are sharing something?* ✔ *What can you do when you are waiting your turn?* ✔ *How can you determine what is okay to share and when it is okay to share?* ✔ *When you ask someone to share with you and they say no, how do you respond?*

★ SKILL STEPS

Sharing Something/Taking Turns

1. Let the other person use the item first.

2. Ask the person if you can use it after they are finished with it.

3. When offered the item, use it for a reasonable amount of time, then give it back or offer it to another person.

NOTE: The skill steps emphasize how to share by taking turns. Adjust the steps as needed if teaching how to share when using an item at the same time.

REASONS

- *Helps you make and keep friends.*
- *Makes it more likely others will share with you.*
- *Makes working and playing with others easier.*

Sharing Something/Taking Turns

LESSON ACTIVITIES AND ASSESSMENTS

- Instruct students to write an entry in their *SEL Journals* describing their use of the skill and what they do when others don't want to share with them.
- Provide students an opportunity to teach the skill to their peers from other classes or students from a lower grade.
- Use the think-pair-share technique. Have students partner up to discuss or role-play how to share or take turns using the following prompts: *If you both want something at the same time, what can you do? What does your voice tone sound like? What does your body language look like?*
- Do a hands-on activity, such as Build a Tower. Ask for a volunteer to help you demonstrate how to share and take turns by building a tower out of blocks. You and the volunteer should take turns adding blocks to the tower. Demonstrate respect and manners by using phrases such as, "Your turn," "Go ahead," and "Thanks, now you can go." After demonstrating how to share and take turns, have another volunteer join you. Continue taking turns and having more students join until everyone is working together and sharing blocks. Keep working together even if the tower falls.

Sharing Something/Taking Turns

MONDAY

- Ask students questions to assess their background knowledge and prior experiences using the skill. Suggested questions can include: *What is something you have shared with someone? Have you ever refused to share something?*
- State the name of the skill, its behavioral steps, and reasons to use the skill.
- Model or demonstrate the skill.
- Have students identify things they can and cannot share when they are in different school environments (playground, cafeteria, library/media center, health office, counseling office, etc.).
- Invite students to practice the skill using the following role-play scenario:
  - *A classmate asks you to share your art supplies with them.*

TUESDAY

- Review the steps of the skill as well as the reasons for using it.
- Identify people, areas, and/or situations where students might use the skill at school (playground, cafeteria, library/media center, health office, counseling office, with a substitute teacher, etc.).
- Explain any behavioral steps or skills which may need to be altered or added for those people, areas, and/or situations.
- Share examples you've witnessed in your classroom of students using the skill.
- Read *All about Sharing* by Bryan Smith, then lead a discussion about how Marcos and Lili learned to compromise and share with each other.
- Assign additional activities to support skill development: DOWNLOADABLE ACTIVITIES: *All about Sharing* by Bryan Smith.
- Invite students to practice the skill with a partner using a role-play scenario they create or one you provide (see appendix).

WEDNESDAY

- Review the steps of the skill as well as the reasons for using it.
- Share examples you've witnessed around school of students using the skill.
- Identify people, areas, and/or situations where students might use the skill at home or with other significant adults or peers (teammates, neighborhood friends, family members/caregivers, etc.).
- Explain any behavioral steps or skills which may need to be altered or added for those people, areas, and/or situations.
- Read *Awesome Dawson It's NOT Your Turn!* by Julia Cook, then lead a class discussion using the following prompts: *What does taking turns mean? How do you take turns in a fair way?*
- Invite students to practice the skill with a partner using a role-play scenario they create or one you provide (see appendix).

Sharing Something/Taking Turns

THURSDAY	▪ Review the steps of the skill as well as the reasons for using it. ▪ Ask students to share examples of how they have used the skill at home or with other adults/peers. ▪ Identify people, areas, and/or situations (store, restaurant, public event, etc.) where students might use the skill in their community. ▪ Explain any behavioral steps or skills which may need to be altered or added for those people, areas, and/or situations. ▪ Instruct students to answer the following question in their *SEL Journals*: *What will you say if someone doesn't want to share something with you?* ▪ Invite students to practice the skill with a partner using a role-play scenario they create or one you provide (see appendix).
FRIDAY	▪ Review the steps of the skill as well as the reasons for using it. ▪ Ask students to share examples of how they have used the skill in their community or with other adults/peers. ▪ Read *Teamwork Isn't My Thing, and I Don't Like to Share!*, then assign additional activities to support skill development using the **Teamwork Isn't My Thing, and I Don't Like to Share! Activity Guide for Teachers** by Julia Cook. ▪ Engage students in discussions about how using the skill has helped them, or in what situations it was difficult. ▪ Encourage students to think about how the skill might be used in a future job/career, hobby, or other area of interest.

Sharing Something/ Taking Turns

1. Let the other person use the item first.

2. Ask the person if you can use it after they are finished with it.

3. When offered the item, use it for a reasonable amount of time, then give it back or offer it to another person.

Talking with Others
(Having a Conversation)

SUGGESTED MATERIALS	■ *Herman Jiggle, Say Hello!* by Julia Cook ■ *Freddie the Fly: Motormouth* and *Freddie the Fly: Motormouth Downloadable Activities* by Kimberly Delude
LESSON OBJECTIVES	■ Recognize how to talk with others and have a conversation in a variety of situations and settings. ■ Determine what the skill of **Talking with Others (Having a Conversation)** looks and sounds like in their classroom. ■ Review prior knowledge and experiences of talking with others and having conversations within the school environment. ■ Analyze community-based situations to identify where, when, and with whom the skill of **Talking with Others (Having a Conversation)** may be used. ■ Evaluate how the skill of **Talking with Others (Having a Conversation)** might apply to various jobs or areas of interest.
ESSENTIAL QUESTIONS	✔ *How do you start a conversation?* ✔ *What is tone of voice? Why is it important?* ✔ *How can you be respectful when having a conversation?* ✔ *What are some words you can say that show manners and respect when talking?* ✔ *Are there times when talking with others should be avoided?* ✔ *When is the best time to talk with others?*

★ **SKILL STEPS**

**Talking with Others
(Having a Conversation)**

1. Look at the person.
2. Use a pleasant voice.
3. Ask questions.
4. Avoid interrupting.

→

REASONS

- *Shows interest in and understanding of others.*
- *Helps you develop and maintain friendships.*
- *Allows you to share your thoughts and opinions.*

Talking with Others
(Having a Conversation)

<table>
<tr>
<td>LESSON ACTIVITIES AND ASSESSMENTS</td>
<td>

- ■ Role-play scenarios (see appendix) that allow students to practice the skill of **Talking with Others (Having a Conversation)** while using different tones of voice (happy, sad, loud, calm, respectful, etc.).
- ■ Instruct students to write in their *SEL Journals* about how they use the skill in school, at home, and in their community.
- ■ Provide students an opportunity to teach the skill to their peers from other classes or students from a lower grade.
- ▶ Watch a video, such as *Kid President's 20 Things We Should Say More Often* video (3:31): https://www.youtube.com/watch?v=m5yCOSHeYn4. Then lead a class discussion by asking students to identify one new thing they will say more often.
- ■ Do a hands-on activity. Create conversation starters by having students write different sentences and conversation starters on note cards. Examples can include:
  - • *Give a compliment: I like your shirt.*
  - • *Offer help: Can I help you? Do you want to borrow mine?*
  - • *Ask a question: Is that a good book? What's your favorite _____________?*
  - • *Acknowledge something about the person: You're good at math. You tell the funniest stories.*
- ■ Lead a class discussion using the following prompt: *In a conversation, what verbal and nonverbal cues can you give to show someone you're listening and paying attention to what they're saying?*
  - • *Nonverbal cues can include: eye contact, head nods, leaning in, sitting up and facing them, etc.*
  - • *Verbal cues can include: "Yes," "Uh-huh," "I see," or asking questions and repeating what was said.*

</td>
</tr>
</table>

Talking with Others (Having a Conversation)

MONDAY	■ Ask students questions to assess their background knowledge and prior experiences using the skill. Suggested questions can include: *What topics are easy for you to talk about with others? What topics are boring for you when talking with others?* ■ State the name of the skill, its behavioral steps, and reasons to use the skill. ■ Model or demonstrate the skill. ■ Have students identify different school environments or situations (playground, cafeteria, library/media center, health office, counseling office, etc.) when it is not okay to talk with others. ■ Invite students to practice the skill using the following role-play scenario: • *A new student joins the class. You are assigned to be their "buddy for the day," helping them and explaining some of the rules. What do you say?*
TUESDAY	■ Review the steps of the skill as well as the reasons for using it. ■ Identify people, areas, and/or situations where students might use the skill at school (playground, cafeteria, library/media center, health office, counseling office, with a substitute teacher, etc.). ■ Explain any behavioral steps or skills which may need to be altered or added for those people, areas, and/or situations. ■ Share examples you've witnessed in your classroom of students using the skill. ■ Read *Herman Jiggle, Say Hello!* by Julia Cook, then lead a discussion about how Herman learned to manage the anxiety he felt when speaking to others. ■ Invite students to practice the skill with a partner using a role-play scenario they create or one you provide (see appendix).
WEDNESDAY	■ Review the steps of the skill as well as the reasons for using it. ■ Share examples you've witnessed around school of students using the skill. ■ Identify people, areas, and/or situations where students might use the skill at home or with other significant adults or peers (teammates, neighborhood friends, family members/caregivers, etc.). ■ Explain any behavioral steps or skills which may need to be altered or added for those people, areas, and/or situations. ▶ Watch a video, such as *Taking Turns Speaking* (2:04): https://www.youtube.com/watch?v=3RjRZ9jMfs0. ■ Use the think-pair-share technique. Have students partner up to discuss or role-play how to talk with others using the following prompt: *Describe or show how to listen and take turns speaking when having a conversation with a new student.*

Talking with Others (Having a Conversation)

THURSDAY	■ Review the steps of the skill as well as the reasons for using it. ■ Ask students to share examples of how they have used the skill at home or with other adults/peers. ■ Identify people, areas, and/or situations (store, restaurant, public event, etc.) where students might use the skill in their community. ■ Explain any behavioral steps or skills which may need to be altered or added for those people, areas, and/or situations. ■ Instruct students to answer the following question in their *SEL Journals: What will you say or do if someone interrupts you?* ■ Invite students to practice the skill with a partner using a role-play scenario they create or one you provide (see appendix).
FRIDAY	■ Review the steps of the skill as well as the reasons for using it. ■ Ask students to share examples of how they have used the skill in their community or with other adults/peers. ■ Read *Freddie the Fly: Motormouth*, then assign additional activities to support skill development: DOWNLOADABLE ACTIVITIES: *Freddie the Fly: Motormouth* by Kimberly Delude. ■ Engage students in discussions about how using the skill has helped them, or in what situations it was difficult. ■ Encourage students to think about how the skill might be used in a future job/career, hobby, or other area of interest.

Talking with Others (Having a Conversation)

1. Look at the person.

2. Use a pleasant voice.

3. Ask questions.

4. Avoid interrupting.

Accepting Compliments

SUGGESTED MATERIALS	■ *Thanks for the Feedback… (I Think?)* and *Thanks for the Feedback… (I Think?) Activity Guide for Teachers* by Julia Cook
LESSON OBJECTIVES	■ Recognize how to accept compliments in a variety of situations and settings. ■ Determine what the skill of **Accepting Compliments** looks and sounds like in their classroom. ■ Demonstrate the skill of **Accepting Compliments** in school, at home, and in other environments. ■ Explore prior knowledge of accepting compliments within the school environment. ■ Analyze community-based situations to identify where, when, and with whom the skill of **Accepting Compliments** may be used. ■ Evaluate how the skill of **Accepting Compliments** might apply to various jobs or areas of interest.
ESSENTIAL QUESTIONS	✔ *Why should your response to a compliment be more than one word?* ✔ *What are some words you can say to acknowledge a compliment?* ✔ *What should your tone of voice sound like when responding to a compliment?* ✔ *Ignoring a compliment should be avoided. Why?* ✔ *When you give a compliment, how do you expect others to respond? Are your expectations reasonable, or do they need adjusting?*

★ **SKILL STEPS**		**REASONS**
Accepting Compliments 1. Look at the person. 2. Use a pleasant voice. 3. Say, "Thank you," "Thanks for noticing," or "I appreciate that." 4. Avoid looking away or denying the compliment.	→	• *Shows respect to the person complimenting you.* • *Improves the chances you'll get more compliments in the future.* • *Shows others you are mature.*

Accepting Compliments

<table>
<tr><td>

LESSON
ACTIVITIES
AND
ASSESSMENTS

</td><td>

- Role-play scenarios (see appendix) that allow students to practice the skill of **Accepting Compliments** while using different tones of voice (happy, mad, sad, loud, calm, respectful, etc.).
- Instruct students to write in their *SEL Journals* about how and when they use the skill and what specific words they say when accepting compliments.
- Provide students an opportunity to teach the skill to their peers from other classes or students from a lower grade.
- Use the think-pair-share technique. Have students partner up to discuss or role-play how to accept compliments using the following prompts: *What was the best compliment you ever received, and how did you react to it? What is the best compliment you ever gave someone, and what did you say to them?*
- Ask students to describe or draw a situation where they did not accept or agree with a compliment they were given. If appropriate, ask for volunteers to share their examples.
- Do a hands-on activity. Pair students together, give each student a sticky note, and then instruct them to write a compliment about their partner on the note. Have the students stand or sit back to back, exchange their sticky notes, and think about how the compliment makes them feel. Next, have the partners face each other and say the compliment out loud. Ask the students if looking at their partners made them feel differently about the compliment. Have students practice appropriate ways to accept compliments. Appropriate responses can include:
  - *Thank you.*
  - *Thanks, that's nice of you to say.*
  - *Smile, nod, and then compliment them back.*

</td></tr>
</table>

Weekly Activities

Accepting Compliments

MONDAY

- Ask students questions to assess their background knowledge and prior experiences using the skill. Suggested questions can include: *Have you ever given a compliment to someone, and they didn't accept it? How did that make you feel? Have you ever given a compliment to someone, and they accepted it? How did that make both of you feel?*
- State the name of the skill, its behavioral steps, and reasons to use the skill.
- Model or demonstrate the skill.
- Have students identify the types of compliments that can be given in different school environments or situations (playground, cafeteria, library/media center, health office, counseling office, etc.).
- Invite students to practice the skill with a partner using the following role-play scenarios:
  - *Someone says they like your new shoes, what do you say?*
  - *Someone says they like your new haircut, even though you don't like it. What do you say?*

TUESDAY

- Review the steps of the skill as well as the reasons for using it.
- Identify people, areas, and/or situations where students might use the skill at school (playground, cafeteria, library/media center, health office, counseling office, with a substitute teacher, etc.).
- Explain any behavioral steps or skills which may need to be altered or added for those people, areas, and/or situations.
- Share examples you've witnessed in your classroom of students using the skill.
- ▶ Watch a video, such as *Accepting Compliments* (4:11): https://www.youtube.com/watch?v=89AfjKXpkkU. Then divide the class into small groups and have each group discuss accepting compliments using the following prompts: *What can you say when you receive a compliment? Why should you not ignore a compliment?*

WEDNESDAY

- Review the steps of the skill as well as the reasons for using it.
- Share examples you've witnessed around school of students using the skill.
- Identify people, areas, and/or situations where students might use the skill at home or with other significant adults or peers (teammates, neighborhood friends, family members/caregivers, etc.).
- Explain any behavioral steps or skills which may need to be altered or added for those people, areas, and/or situations.
- ▶ Watch a video, such as *How to Give and Receive a Compliment* (3:16): https://www.youtube.com/watch?v=Fne1gW4nQSs.
- Use the Give One, Get One discussion strategy (sharing and seeking information with one another) and ask students the following question: *Why should you respond with more than one word when you receive a compliment?*

Accepting Compliments

THURSDAY	■ Review the steps of the skill as well as the reasons for using it. ■ Ask students to share examples of how they have used the skill at home or with other adults/peers. ■ Identify people, areas, and/or situations (store, restaurant, public event, etc.) where students might use the skill in their community. ■ Explain any behavioral steps or skills which may need to be altered or added for those people, areas, and/or situations. ■ Instruct students to answer the following questions in their *SEL Journals*: *When I give a compliment, how do I expect others to respond? Are my expectations reasonable, or do they need adjusting?* ■ Invite students to practice the skill with a partner using a role-play scenario they create or one you provide (see appendix).
FRIDAY	■ Review the steps of the skill as well as the reasons for using it. ■ Ask students to share examples of how they have used the skill in their community or with other adults/peers. ■ Read ***Thanks for the Feedback... (I Think?)***, then assign additional activities to support skill development using the ***Thanks for the Feedback... (I Think?) Activity Guide for Teachers*** by Julia Cook. ■ Engage students in discussions about how using the skill has helped them, or in what situations it was difficult. ■ Encourage students to think about how the skill might be used in a future job/career, hobby, or other area of interest.

Accepting Compliments

1. Look at the person.

2. Use a pleasant voice.

3. Say, "Thank you," "Thanks for noticing," or "I appreciate that."

4. Avoid looking away or denying the compliment.

Using Technology Appropriately (in School)

SUGGESTED MATERIALS	■ *The Technology Tail* by Julia Cook ■ *Zombie Phone Kids* by Michael Garland
LESSON OBJECTIVES	■ Recognize appropriate use of technology in a variety of situations and settings. ■ Describe what using technology appropriately looks like in their classroom. ■ Demonstrate the skill of **Using Technology Appropriately**. ■ Examine how the skill can be used at home and with adults/peers in other settings. ■ Analyze community-based situations to identify where, when, and with whom the skill of **Using Technology Appropriately** may be used. ■ Evaluate how the skill of **Using Technology Appropriately** might apply to various careers or areas of interest.
ESSENTIAL QUESTIONS	✔ *What social media do you use?* ✔ *How can you determine appropriate use of technology (safe vs. unsafe)?* ✔ *What are your favorite online video games to play?* ✔ *What are some different ways you can determine if your technology use is appropriate?* ✔ *Who in school, at home, or in your community is a trusted adult you can go to if you need to report something?* ✔ *How can you make sure your online activities are appropriate?*

★ SKILL STEPS

Using Technology Appropriately (in School)

1. Follow any rules or expectations set for you related to the use of technology.

2. Access only appropriate or designated programs or websites, avoiding those that promote violence, intolerance, or explicit language and images.

3. Avoid reading or posting negative, harmful, or offensive messages about others and sharing personal information online.

4. If you find yourself in a dangerous or uncomfortable situation, report it to a trusted adult.

REASONS

- *Keeps you safe.*
- *Allows you to continue to have access to the technology.*

Using Technology Appropriately (in School)

LESSON ACTIVITIES AND ASSESSMENTS

▶ Provide students and families resources to help them find age-appropriate video games:
https://www.commonsensemedia.org/game-reviews
https://www.esrb.org (Entertainment Software Rating Board).

■ Instruct students to write in their *SEL Journals* about how they use the skill and what specifically was the most challenging step for them.

■ Provide students an opportunity to teach the skill to their peers from other classes or students from a lower grade.

■ Use the think-pair-share technique. Have students partner up to discuss or role-play how to use technology appropriately using the following prompt: *What are some of the potential dangers of using technology?*

■ Ask students to describe or draw a situation where they did not follow the rules for using technology appropriately, and what happened as a result. If appropriate, ask for volunteers to share their examples.

Using Technology Appropriately (in School)

MONDAY

- Ask students questions to assess their background knowledge and prior experiences using the skill. Suggested questions can include: *Do you know what the rules are for using technology at school? At home? Why is it important for you to be a responsible user of technology?*
- State the name of the skill, its behavioral steps, and reasons to use the skill.
- Model or demonstrate the skill.
- Have students identify the type of technology use that occurs in different school environments (playground, cafeteria, library/media center, health office, counseling office, etc.).
- Invite students to practice the skill using a role-play scenario you provide (see appendix).
- Do a safety-themed activity. Share with students the following examples and ask them to choose whether it is safe or not safe.
  - *Robbie posts a family vacation photo on Instagram. It does not reveal their location.* **SAFE** or **NOT SAFE**
  - *Reyna sends the following group text: Party @ my house Sat 6 pm 105 Arrowlane Drive… spread the word* **SAFE** or **NOT SAFE**

TUESDAY

- Review the steps of the skill as well as the reasons for using it.
- Read *The Technology Tail* by Julia Cook, then divide the class into small groups and have each group discuss the story using the following prompts: *What does it mean to have a digital trail? How can you make sure your digital trail is a positive one? What should you do when you're not sure if something you want to post online is appropriate or helpful?*
- Share examples you've witnessed in your classroom of students using the skill.

WEDNESDAY

- Review the steps of the skill as well as the reasons for using it.
- Share examples you've witnessed around school of students using the skill.
- Identify people, areas, and/or situations where students might use the skill at home or with other significant adults or peers (teammates, neighborhood friends, family members/caregivers, etc.).
- Explain any behavioral steps or skills which may need to be altered or added for those people, areas, and/or situations.
- Do a safety-themed activity. Have students work with the person seated next to them (shoulder/elbow partner) and decide if the following examples are safe or not safe.
  - *On Instagram, someone posts an "I'm bored" selfie with the message: "Text me I am bored 555-555-5555!* **SAFE** or **NOT SAFE**
  - *On Snapchat, Molly posts a selfie with the caption: "Feeling all alone @ 1220 Cypress Ln"* **SAFE** or **NOT SAFE**
- Use the Give One, Get One discussion strategy (sharing and seeking information with one another) and ask students the following question: *How can you make sure you act responsibly and appropriately online?*

Using Technology Appropriately (in School)

THURSDAY	■ Review the steps of the skill as well as the reasons for using it. ■ Ask students to share examples of how they have used the skill at home or with other adults/peers. ■ Identify people, areas, and/or situations (store, restaurant, public event, etc.) where students might use the skill in their community. ■ Explain any behavioral steps or skills which may need to be altered or added for those people, areas, and/or situations. ■ Instruct students to answer the following question in their *SEL Journals*: *Who in school, at home, or in the community is a trusted adult I can go to if I need to report something that happened online?*
FRIDAY	■ Review the steps of the skill as well as the reasons for using it. ■ Ask students to share examples of how they have used the skill in their community or with other adults/peers. ■ Read ***Zombie Phone Kids***, then assign additional activities to support skill development: DOWNLOADABLE ACTIVITIES: ***Zombie Phone Kids*** by Michael Garland. ■ Encourage students to think about how the skill might be used in a future job/career, hobby, or other area of interest.

Using Technology Appropriately (in School)

1. Follow any rules or expectations set for you related to the use of technology.

2. Access only appropriate or designated programs or websites, avoiding those that promote violence, intolerance, or explicit language and images.

3. Avoid reading or posting negative, harmful, or offensive messages about others and sharing personal information online.

4. If you find yourself in a dangerous or uncomfortable situation, report it to a trusted adult.

Asking for Clarification

SUGGESTED MATERIALS	■ *Defining the Problem (13 & Counting: Rescue Me?)* downloadable activity by Tamara Zentic ■ *What's the Problem?* and *What's the Problem? Downloadable Activities* by Bryan Smith
LESSON OBJECTIVES	■ Recognize how to ask for clarification in a variety of situations and settings. ■ Determine what asking for clarification looks and sounds like in their classroom. ■ Review prior knowledge about asking for clarification within the school environment. ■ Demonstrate the skill of **Asking for Clarification** in school, at home, and in their community. ■ Analyze community-based situations to identify where, when, and with whom the skill of **Asking for Clarification** may be used. ■ Evaluate how the skill of **Asking for Clarification** might apply to various jobs or areas of interest.
ESSENTIAL QUESTIONS	✔ *What does asking for clarification sound like?* ✔ *How do you know when you should ask for clarification?* ✔ *How can you ask for clarification in a respectful way?* ✔ *What are some words you can say to show manners and respect when asking someone for more information?* ✔ *When you need more clarification, who is the best person to ask?* ✔ *When is the best time to ask for clarification?*

★ SKILL STEPS

Asking for Clarification

1. Look at the person.
2. Ask if they have time to talk.
3. Use a pleasant or neutral voice.
4. State specifically what you are confused about.
5. Listen to the person's reply and ask questions if needed.
6. Thank the person for their time.

→

REASONS

- *Helps clear up any confusion.*
- *Makes misunderstandings less likely.*
- *Improves communication.*

Asking for Clarification

LESSON ACTIVITIES AND ASSESSMENTS

- Instruct students to write in their *SEL Journals* about how they use the skill and what specific words they say when they need more clarification.
- Provide students an opportunity to teach the skill to their peers from other classes or students from a lower grade.
- Use the think-pair-share technique. Have students partner up to discuss or role-play asking for clarification using the following prompt: *How do you know when you should ask for clarification?*
- Ask students to describe or draw a situation where they did not ask for clarification even though they were confused or unsure. If appropriate, ask for volunteers to share their examples.
- Do a group activity. Show an image of a space alien along with a variety of everyday objects. Explain to students that this alien has come to earth and doesn't know the English-language word for certain things. Have students try to figure out what the alien is requesting by asking for more clarification and understanding. For example, the alien might ask, "Can I have the kazooble, please?" In response, students will need to ask clarifying questions to determine which item the alien called a kazooble.

Asking for Clarification

MONDAY

- Have students identify what types of clarification may be needed in different school environments or situations (playground, cafeteria, library/media center, health office, counseling office, etc.).
- State the name of the skill, its behavioral steps, and reasons to use the skill.
- Model or demonstrate the skill.
- Invite students to practice the skill with a partner using the following role-play scenario:
  - *You are listening to the teacher give instructions but think you may have missed one. What do you say and to whom?*

TUESDAY

- Review the steps of the skill as well as the reasons for using it.
- Identify people, areas, and/or situations where students might use the skill at school (playground, cafeteria, library/media center, health office, counseling office, with a substitute teacher, etc.).
- Explain any behavioral steps or skills which may need to be altered or added for those people, areas, and/or situations.
- Share examples you've witnessed in your classroom of students using the skill.
- ▶ Watch a video, such as *How Miscommunication Happens (and How to Avoid It)* (4:32): https://www.youtube.com/watch?v=gCfzeONu3Mo, then use the think-pair-share technique. Have students partner up to discuss or role-play two things they learned from watching the video.

WEDNESDAY

- Review the steps of the skill as well as the reasons for using it.
- Share examples you've witnessed around school of students using the skill.
- Identify people, areas, and/or situations where students might use the skill at home or with other significant adults or peers (teammates, neighborhood friends, family members/caregivers, etc.).
- Explain any behavioral steps or skills which may need to be altered or added for those people, areas, and/or situations.
- Divide the class into small discussion groups and give them the following prompt:
  - *Talking to someone is like playing catch back and forth. Sometimes we drop the ball or get distracted. When you don't hear or understand a message, how can you get more clarification? What words can you say that are polite? What is a rude way of asking someone to repeat or clarify what they said?*

Asking for Clarification

THURSDAY

- Review the steps of the skill as well as the reasons for using it.
- Ask students to share examples of how they have used the skill at home or with other adults/peers.
- Identify people, areas, and/or situations (store, restaurant, public event, etc.) where students might use the skill in their community.
- Explain any behavioral steps or skills which may need to be altered or added for those people, areas, and/or situations.
- Instruct students to write in their *SEL Journals* about a time when they asked someone for more clarification. Then ask them to answer the following question: *When is the best time to ask for clarification?*
- Read *What's the Problem?*, then assign additional activities to support skill development: DOWNLOADABLE ACTIVITIES: *What's the Problem?* by Bryan Smith.
+ Extend the learning by discussing helpful strategies, such as:
  - *Be an active listener. Active listening involves focusing your eyes, ears, brain, and body.*
  - *Try to understand what someone is saying.*
  - *Use clarifying statements, such as, "This is how I see it. What do you see?"*

FRIDAY

- Review the steps of the skill as well as the reasons for using it.
- Invite students to practice the skill of **Asking for Clarification** with a partner using different tones of voice (mad, sad, loud, calm, respectful, etc.). Have them use a role-play scenario they create or one you provide (see appendix).
- Ask students to share examples of how they have used the skill in their community or with other adults/peers.
- Encourage students to think about how the skill might be used in a future job/career, hobby, or other area of interest.
- Assign additional activities to support skill development: DOWNLOADABLE ACTIVITY: *Defining the Problem (13 & Counting: Rescue Me?)* by Tamara Zentic.

Asking for Clarification

1. Look at the person.

2. Ask if they have time to talk.

3. Use a pleasant or neutral voice.

4. State specifically what you are confused about.

5. Listen to the person's reply and ask questions if needed.

6. Thank the person for their time.

Correcting Another Person (Giving Criticism/Feedback)

SUGGESTED MATERIALS	■ *I Can't Believe You Said That!* and *I Can't Believe You Said That! Activity Guide for Teachers* by Julia Cook ■ *Freddie the Fly: Truth or Care* and *Freddie the Fly: Truth or Care Downloadable Activities* by Kimberly Delude
LESSON OBJECTIVES	■ Recognize how to correct another person in a variety of situations and settings. ■ Determine what correcting another person looks and sounds like in their classroom. ■ Demonstrate the skill of **Correcting Another Person (Giving Criticism/Feedback)** in school, at home, and in their community. ■ Review prior knowledge of correcting another person within the school environment. ■ Analyze community-based situations to identify where, when, and with whom the skill of **Correcting Another Person (Giving Criticism/Feedback)** may be used. ■ Evaluate how the skill of **Correcting Another Person (Giving Criticism/Feedback)** might apply to various jobs or areas of interest.
ESSENTIAL QUESTIONS	✔ *What does correcting another person sound and look like?* ✔ *How do you know when you need to correct another person?* ✔ *How can you give feedback or correct another person in a respectful way?* ✔ *What are some words you can use to show manners and respect when giving criticism or feedback?* ✔ *When is the best time to correct another person?* ✔ *When you correct another person, how do you expect them to respond? Are your expectations reasonable, or do they need adjusting?*

★ SKILL STEPS

Correcting Another Person (Giving Criticism/Feedback)

1. Look at the person.
2. Remain calm and use a pleasant voice tone.
3. Begin with a positive statement or by saying, "I understand…."
4. Clearly describe your concern.
5. Give a reason.
6. Listen to the person's explanation, avoiding sarcasm, name-calling, or put-downs.

→

REASONS

- *Helps others improve their work.*
- *Keeps others safe or from repeating mistakes.*

Correcting Another Person (Giving Criticism/Feedback)

LESSON ACTIVITIES AND ASSESSMENTS

- Instruct students to write in their *SEL Journals* about how they use the skill and what specific words they say when correcting another person.
- Provide students an opportunity to teach the skill to their peers from other classes or students from a lower grade.
- Role-play scenarios (see appendix) that allow students to practice the skill while using different tones of voice (mad, loud, quiet, sad, calm, etc.).
- Use the think-pair-share technique. Have students partner up to discuss the skill of **Correcting Another Person (Giving Criticism/Feedback)** using the following prompt: *How do you know when you should correct another person?*
- Ask students to write about or draw a situation where they corrected someone or gave them feedback in an inappropriate way. Or, have them describe or draw a situation where they did not accept feedback or a criticism in an appropriate way. If appropriate, ask for volunteers to share their examples.
- Share tips to expand students' understanding of the skill, including HOW, WHEN, and WHEN NOT to correct someone. You might say the following: "Correcting someone over something small or unimportant is usually not necessary and not worth the embarrassment it may cause them (or you)."
- Additional tips you can mention include the following:
  - *Correcting someone by saying, "Um, actually…." is not the best way to begin. A better option is to say something like, "Excuse me, but did you mean to say…."*
  - *Correct privately.*
  - *Use a gentle or neutral voice tone.*
  - *Explain why you felt the correction was needed. (Children, family, relatives, friends, and employees are examples of groups you have a responsibility and/or the ability to correct.)*
- Share an example of how to correct someone who says the wrong word. Here is an example:
  - A classmate says, *"The teacher **taked** her to the nurse's office."* You respond by…
    - *Repeating what you heard and saying it correctly. "Oh. The teacher **took** her to the nurse's office. Why? What happened?"*
    - *Asking the person to explain it to you. "Hmmm. I don't understand. Can you explain it to me?" or "That doesn't make sense to me. What do you mean?"*
  - A classmate does something incorrectly. You respond by…
    - *Pointing out what is not correct and asking if there's another way to do it.*

Correcting Another Person (Giving Criticism/Feedback)

MONDAY	<ul><li>Have students identify when it is NOT okay to correct another person in various school environments (playground, cafeteria, library/media center, health office, counseling office, etc.).</li><li>State the name of the skill, its behavioral steps, and reasons to use the skill.</li><li>Model or demonstrate the skill.</li><li>Invite students to practice the skill with a partner using the following role-play scenario:<ul><li>*A classmate keeps saying your name wrong, and you are not sure if it is a mistake or on purpose. How do you correct them?*</li></ul></li></ul>
TUESDAY	<ul><li>Review the steps of the skill as well as the reasons for using it.</li><li>Identify people, areas, and/or situations where students might use the skill at school (playground, cafeteria, library/media center, health office, counseling office, with a substitute teacher, etc.).</li><li>Explain any behavioral steps or skills which may need to be altered or added for those people, areas, and/or situations.</li><li>Share examples you've witnessed in your classroom of students using the skill.</li><li>Use the think-pair-share technique. Have students partner up to discuss the skill using the following prompts: *Why is it important to know how to correct others? In what types of situations is it hard to correct someone? In what types of situations is it easy to correct someone?*</li></ul>
WEDNESDAY	<ul><li>Review the steps of the skill as well as the reasons for using it.</li><li>Share examples you've witnessed around school of students using the skill.</li><li>Identify people, areas, and/or situations where students might use the skill at home or with other significant adults or peers (teammates, neighborhood friends, family members/caregivers, etc.).</li><li>Explain any behavioral steps or skills which may need to be altered or added for those people, areas, and/or situations.</li><li>Read *Freddie the Fly: Truth or Care*, then assign additional activities to support skill development: DOWNLOADABLE ACTIVITIES: *Freddie the Fly: Truth or Care* by Kimberly Delude.</li><li>Divide the class into small discussion groups and give them the following prompt:<ul><li>*How can you correct another person in a respectful way?*</li></ul></li></ul>

Correcting Another Person (Giving Criticism/Feedback)

THURSDAY	■ Review the steps of the skill as well as the reasons for using it. ■ Ask students to share examples of how they have used the skill at home or with other adults/peers. ■ Identify people, areas, and/or situations (store, restaurant, public event, etc.) where students might use the skill in their community. ■ Explain any behavioral steps or skills which may need to be altered or added for those people, areas, and/or situations. ■ Instruct students to write in their *SEL Journals* answers to the following questions: *When I am correcting another person, how do I expect them to respond? Are my expectations reasonable, or do they need adjusting?* ■ Invite students to practice the skill with a partner using a role-play scenario they create or one you provide (see appendix).
FRIDAY	■ Review the steps of the skill as well as the reasons for using it. ■ Invite students to practice the skill of **Correcting Another Person (Giving Criticism/ Feedback)** with a partner using different tones of voice (mad, sad, loud, calm, respectful, etc.). Have them use a role-play scenario they create or one you provide (see appendix). ■ Ask students to share examples of how they have used the skill in their community or with other adults/peers. ■ Encourage students to think about how the skill might be used in a future job/career, hobby, or other area of interest. ■ Read *I Can't Believe You Said That!*, then assign additional activities to support skill development using the *I Can't Believe You Said That! Activity Guide for Teachers* by Julia Cook.

Correcting Another Person (Giving Criticism/Feedback)

1. Look at the person.

2. Remain calm and use a pleasant voice tone.

3. Begin with a positive statement or by saying, "I understand…."

4. Clearly describe your concern.

5. Give a reason.

6. Listen to the person's explanation, avoiding sarcasm, name-calling, or put-downs.

Accepting Apologies from Others

SUGGESTED MATERIALS	■ *When Sophie's Sorry Wasn't Enough* by Jeff Tucker
LESSON OBJECTIVES	■ Recognize how to accept apologies from others in a variety of situations and settings. ■ Determine what accepting apologies looks and sounds like in their classroom. ■ Demonstrate the skill of **Accepting Apologies from Others** in school, at home, and in other environments. ■ Review prior knowledge of accepting apologies from others within the school environment. ■ Analyze community-based situations to identify where, when, and with whom the skill of **Accepting Apologies from Others** may be used. ■ Evaluate how the skill of **Accepting Apologies from Others** might apply to various jobs or areas of interest.
ESSENTIAL QUESTIONS	✔ *What does accepting apologies from others look and sound like?* ✔ *How do you know when you need to accept an apology from someone?* ✔ *How can you show respect when accepting apologies from others?* ✔ *What are some words you can say to show manners and respect when accepting apologies from others?* ✔ *When is the best time to accept an apology?* ✔ *When you accept apologies from others, how do you expect them to respond? Are your expectations reasonable, or do they need adjusting?*

★ SKILL STEPS

Accepting Apologies from Others

1. Look at the person who is apologizing.
2. Listen to what they are saying without interrupting.
3. Remain calm. Refrain from making sarcastic statements.
4. Say, "I accept your apology" or "Thank you for apologizing."

→

REASONS

- *Helps repair friendships and relationships.*
- *Allows you to move on and not stay stuck in the past.*

Accepting Apologies from Others

LESSON ACTIVITIES AND ASSESSMENTS	■ Instruct students to write in their *SEL Journals* about how they use the skill and what specific words they say when accepting an apology. ■ Provide students an opportunity to teach the skill to their peers from other classes or students from a lower grade. ■ Role-play scenarios (see appendix) that allow students to practice the skill while using different tones of voice (mad, loud, quiet, sad, calm, etc.). ■ Use the think-pair-share technique. Have students partner up to discuss or role-play giving and accepting apologies using the following prompt: *How do you know when to give and when to accept an apology?*

Accepting Apologies from Others

MONDAY

- Have students identify when they may need to accept an apology in various school environments (playground, cafeteria, library/media center, health office, counseling office, etc.).
- State the name of the skill, its behavioral steps, and reasons to use the skill.
- Model or demonstrate the skill.
- Invite students to practice the skill with a partner using the following role-play scenario:
  - *A classmate spills milk on your pants by accident, and now your pants look and feel wet. When she says, "Sorry!" what do you say and do?*

TUESDAY

- Review the steps of the skill as well as the reasons for using it.
- Identify people, areas, and/or situations where students might use the skill at school (playground, cafeteria, library/media center, health office, counseling office, with a substitute teacher, etc.).
- Explain any behavioral steps or skills which may need to be altered or added for those people, areas, and/or situations.
- Share examples you've witnessed in your classroom of students using the skill.
- Use the think-pair-share technique. Have students partner up to discuss or role-play the skill using the following prompt: *Besides saying, "It's okay," what are other responses when accepting an apology?*

WEDNESDAY

- Review the steps of the skill as well as the reasons for using it.
- Share examples you've witnessed around school of students using the skill.
- Identify people, areas, and/or situations where students might use the skill at home or with other significant adults or peers (teammates, neighborhood friends, family members/caregivers, etc.).
- Explain any behavioral steps or skills which may need to be altered or added for those people, areas, and/or situations.
- ▶ Watch a video, such as *What Is Forgiveness?* (2:20): https://www.youtube.com/watch?v=FFuHL6Izk6E.
- Divide the class into small discussion groups and give them the following prompt:
  - *How can you accept an apology in a respectful way?*

Accepting Apologies from Others

<table>
<tr><td>THURSDAY</td><td>

- Review the steps of the skill as well as the reasons for using it.
- Ask students to share examples of how they have used the skill at home or with other adults/peers.
- Identify people, areas, and/or situations (store, restaurant, public event, etc.) where students might use the skill in their community.
- Explain any behavioral steps or skills which may need to be altered or added for those people, areas, and/or situations.
- ▶ Watch a video, such as *Toolbox: Apology and Forgiveness** (13:12): https://www.youtube.com/watch?v=tTifJOPCz7k.
  Note: A lengthier video, it combines a storybook read-aloud with a lesson.
- Divide the class into small discussion groups and give them the following prompt:
  - *What is one thing you learned from the* Toolbox: Apology and Forgiveness *video?*

</td></tr>
<tr><td>FRIDAY</td><td>

- Review the steps of the skill as well as the reasons for using it.
- Invite students to practice the skill with a partner using a role-play scenario they create or one you provide (see appendix). Have them practice the skill while using different tones of voice (mad, loud, quiet, sad, calm, etc.).
- Ask students to share examples of how they have used the skill in their community or with other adults/peers.
- Read **When Sophie's Sorry Wasn't Enough,** then assign additional activities to support skill development: DOWNLOADABLE ACTIVITIES: **When Sophie's Sorry Wasn't Enough** by Jeff Tucker.
- Encourage students to think about how the skill might be used in a future job/career, hobby, or other area of interest.

</td></tr>
</table>

Accepting Apologies from Others

1. Look at the person who is apologizing.

2. Listen to what they are saying without interrupting.

3. Remain calm. Refrain from making sarcastic statements.

4. Say, "I accept your apology" or "Thank you for apologizing."

Showing Appreciation

SUGGESTED MATERIALS	■ *The Power of an Attitude of Gratitude* and *The Power of an Attitude of Gratitude Downloadable Activity Guide* by Kip "Mr. J" Jones ■ *Joy! You Find What You Look For* and *Joy! You Find What You Look For Downloadable Activity Journal* by Gina Prosch
LESSON OBJECTIVES	■ Recognize how to show appreciation in a variety of situations and settings. ■ Determine what showing appreciation looks and sounds like in their classroom. ■ Demonstrate the skill of **Showing Appreciation** in school, at home, and in other environments. ■ Review prior knowledge of showing appreciation within the school environment. ■ Analyze community-based situations to identify where, when, and with whom the skill of **Showing Appreciation** may be used. ■ Evaluate how the skill of **Showing Appreciation** might apply to various jobs or areas of interest.
ESSENTIAL QUESTIONS	✔ *What does showing appreciation sound and look like?* ✔ *How do you know when it's appropriate to show appreciation?* ✔ *How can you show appreciation in a genuine way?* ✔ *Why is it important to show appreciation?* ✔ *When is the best time to show appreciation?* ✔ *When you show appreciation, how do you expect others to respond? Are your expectations reasonable, or do they need adjusting?*

★ SKILL STEPS

Showing Appreciation

1. Look at the person.
2. Use a pleasant, sincere voice.
3. Say, "Thank you for…" and specifically describe what you appreciate.
4. Give a reason why what the person did was so beneficial.
5. Offer to return the favor or help the person in the future (if appropriate).

REASONS

- *Boosts feelings of self-worth.*
- *Makes you feel happiness.*
- *Strengthens friendships.*

+ SKILL EXTENSION:

Giving Compliments

Showing Appreciation

LESSON ACTIVITIES AND ASSESSMENTS

- Role-play scenarios (see appendix) that allow students to practice the skills of **Showing Appreciation** and **Giving Compliments** while using different tones of voice (mad, sad, loud, calm, respectful, etc.).
- Instruct students to write in their *SEL Journals* about how they use both skills and what specific words they say when showing appreciation and giving compliments.
- Provide students an opportunity to teach the skills to their peers from other classes or students from a lower grade.
- Use the think-pair-share technique. Have students partner up to discuss or role-play showing appreciation and giving compliments using the following prompts: *How do you feel when you give a compliment? How do you feel when you receive a compliment? What is the best compliment you ever received?*
- Instruct students to write about or draw in their *SEL Journals* a situation where they did not show appreciation in an appropriate way. Ask for volunteers to share their experiences with the class, if appropriate.
- Assign a daily journal activity. Have students answer one prompt every day for a week, using the following seven prompts:
  - *Write three good things about today.*
  - *Write three things that make you happy.*
  - *Write three things you're grateful for in life.*
  - *Write three things someone has (or others have) done for you that makes you thankful. Or, write three things you would like them to do for you that would make you thankful.*
  - *Write three ways you can show your appreciation to others.*
  - *Write three kind things you can say to others.*
  - *Write three things you appreciate about school.*

Showing Appreciation

MONDAY

- Have students identify when they may need to show appreciation in various school environments (playground, cafeteria, library/media center, health office, counseling office, etc.).
- State the name of the skill, its behavioral steps, and reasons to use the skill.
- Model or demonstrate the skill.
- Invite students to practice the skill with a partner using the following role-play scenario:
  - *Your classmate let you borrow a pencil because you forgot to bring one to class. How do you show your appreciation?*

TUESDAY

- Review the steps of the skill as well as the reasons for using it.
- ▶ Watch a video, such as *Thankful by the Juicebox Jukebox/2021 Gratitude Appreciation Kids Songs Music Thanksgiving* (3:46): https://www.youtube.com/watch?v=YeSdQmO51Ps&t=7s.
- Identify people, areas, and/or situations where students might use the skill at school (playground, cafeteria, library/media center, health office, counseling office, with a substitute teacher, etc.).
- Explain any behavioral steps or skills which may need to be altered or added for those people, areas, and/or situations.
- Share examples you've witnessed in your classroom of students using the skill.
- Use the think-pair-share technique. Have students partner up to discuss or role-play the skill using the following prompt: *Why is it important to show appreciation?*

WEDNESDAY

- Review the steps of the skill as well as the reasons for using it.
- Share examples you've witnessed around school of students using the skill.
- Identify people, areas, and/or situations where students might use the skill at home or with other significant adults or peers (teammates, neighborhood friends, family members/caregivers, etc.).
- Explain any behavioral steps or skills which may need to be altered or added for those people, areas, and/or situations.
- Divide the class into small discussion groups and give them the following prompts:
  - *When do you show appreciation?*
  - *How can you show appreciation in a genuine or real way?*
- Read ***The Power of an Attitude of Gratitude***, then assign additional activities to support skill development: DOWNLOADABLE ACTIVITIES: ***The Power of an Attitude of Gratitude Downloadable Activity Guide*** by Kip "Mr. J" Jones.

Showing Appreciation

THURSDAY	■ Review the steps of the skill as well as the reasons for using it. ■ Ask students to share examples of how they have used the skill at home or with other adults/peers. ■ Identify people, areas, and/or situations (store, restaurant, public event, etc.) where students might use the skill in their community. ■ Explain any behavioral steps or skills which may need to be altered or added for those people, areas, and/or situations. ■ Read *Joy! You Find What You Look For*, then assign additional activities to support skill development: DOWNLOADABLE ACTIVITY JOURNAL: *Joy! You Find What You Look For* by Gina Prosch. ✚ Extend the learning by introducing the skill of **Giving Compliments** and its behavioral steps. Explain how this skill complements the skill of **Showing Appreciation** and how both skills can be used in school, at home, and in the community. **Giving Compliments** skill steps: 1. Look at the person. 2. Use a clear, enthusiastic voice. 3. Praise the person's actions or efforts specifically. 4. Avoid comments that could make others uncomfortable. 5. Give the other person time to respond to your compliment.
FRIDAY	■ Review the steps of both skills as well as the reasons for using them. ■ Ask students to share examples of how they have used either skill in their community. ■ Engage students in discussions about how the skill of **Showing Appreciation** or the skill of **Giving Compliments** has helped them, or in what situations it was difficult. ■ Encourage students to think about how both skills might be used in a future job/career, hobby, or other area of interest.

Showing Appreciation

1. Look at the person.

2. Use a pleasant, sincere voice.

3. Say, "Thank you for…" and specifically describe what you appreciate.

4. Give a reason why what the person did was so beneficial.

5. Offer to return the favor or help the person in the future (if appropriate).

Giving Compliments

1. Look at the person.

2. Use a clear, enthusiastic voice.

3. Praise the person's actions or efforts specifically.

4. Avoid comments that could make others uncomfortable.

5. Give the other person time to respond to your compliment.

Contributing to a Discussion (Joining in a Conversation)

SUGGESTED MATERIALS	■ *Herman Jiggle, Say Hello!* by Julia Cook ■ *Freddie the Fly: Motormouth* and *Freddie the Fly: Motormouth Downloadable Activities* by Kimberly Delude
LESSON OBJECTIVES	■ Recognize how to contribute to a discussion in a variety of situations and settings. ■ Determine what contributing to discussions look and sound like in their classroom. ■ Demonstrate the skill of **Contributing to a Discussion (Joining in a Conversation)** in school, at home, and in other environments. ■ Review prior knowledge of contributing to discussions/joining conversations within the school environment. ■ Analyze community-based situations to identify where, when, and with whom the skill of **Contributing to a Discussion (Joining in a Conversation)** may be used. ■ Evaluate how the skill of **Contributing to a Discussion (Joining in a Conversation)** might apply to various jobs or areas of interest.
ESSENTIAL QUESTIONS	✔ *What does contributing to discussions/joining conversations sound and look like?* ✔ *How do you know when you need to contribute to a discussion?* ✔ *How can you contribute to a discussion in a respectful way?* ✔ *What are some words you can say to show manners and respect when contributing to discussions?* ✔ *When is the best time to contribute to a discussion?* ✔ *When you contribute to a discussion or join a conversation, how do you expect others to respond? Are your expectations reasonable, or do they need adjusting?*

★ SKILL STEPS

Contributing to a Discussion (Joining in a Conversation)

1. Approach the group (or people in conversation) quietly.
2. Look at the person speaking and listen to what is being talked about.
3. Keep a relaxed, attentive posture and nod your head to show interest.
4. Wait for a pause before making any comments.
5. Share something related to the topic, without exaggerating or dominating the conversation.

→

REASONS

- *Helps you learn new things or get answers you need.*
- *Helps you make friends.*

Contributing to a Discussion (Joining in a Conversation)

<table>
<tr><td valign="top">

LESSON ACTIVITIES AND ASSESSMENTS

</td><td valign="top">

- Role-play scenarios (see appendix) that allow students to practice the skill of **Contributing to a Discussion (Joining in a Conversation)** while using different tones of voice (mad, sad, loud, calm, respectful, etc.).
- Instruct students to write in their *SEL Journals* about how they use the skill and what specific words they say when contributing to discussions/joining conversations.
- Provide students an opportunity to teach the skill to their peers from other classes or students from a lower grade.
- Use the think-pair-share technique. Have students partner up to discuss or role-play how to contribute to discussions using the following prompt: *How do you know when you should join in a conversation?*
- Instruct students to write about or draw in their *SEL Journals* a situation where they did not contribute to a discussion in an appropriate way. Ask for volunteers to share their experiences with the class, if appropriate.
- *Read Herman Jiggle, Say Hello!* and *Freddie the Fly: Motormouth* (and corresponding activities). Both storybooks are included in the **Talking with Others (Having a Conversation)** lesson. If you have already read the stories, you can review them again or choose alternative reading activities.

</td></tr>
</table>

Contributing to a Discussion (Joining in a Conversation)

MONDAY

- Have students identify when it is NOT OKAY to contribute to discussions or join conversations in various school situations or settings (playground, cafeteria, library/media center, health office, counseling office, with a substitute teacher, etc.).
- State the name of the skill, its behavioral steps, and reasons to use the skill.
- Model or demonstrate the skill.
- Invite students to practice the skill with a partner using the following prompts and role-play scenarios:
  - *Tell a related story about yourself, such as, "Something almost exactly like that happened to me, too. I was…."*
  - *Show agreement. "Yes, I have done that too," or "Yes, I have seen that too."*
  - *Ask a question, such as, "What was your favorite thing or experience there?"*
  - *Respond to the words of others by saying something such as, "That reminds me of…."*
  - *Ask "why" questions. (This question can reveal an individual's motivation or thinking.)*
  - *Join in a group discussion by asking, "How do you all know each other?"*
  - *Start a discussion with an individual by asking a question, such as, "So, what's your story?"*
  - *To keep a conversation going and demonstrate you're listening, repeat back the last few words you hear someone say.*

TUESDAY

- Review the steps of the skill as well as the reasons for using it.
- Identify people, areas, and/or situations where students might use the skill at school (playground, cafeteria, library/media center, health office, counseling office, with a substitute teacher, etc.).
- Explain any behavioral steps or skills which may need to be altered or added for those people, areas, and/or situations.
- Share examples you've witnessed in your classroom of students using the skill.
- Use the think-pair-share technique. Have students partner up to discuss or role-play the skill using the following prompt: *Why is it important to know how to join a conversation?*

WEDNESDAY

- Review the steps of the skill as well as the reasons for using it.
- Share examples you've witnessed around school of students using the skill.
- Identify people, areas, and/or situations where students might use the skill at home or with other significant adults or peers (teammates, neighborhood friends, family members/caregivers, etc.).
- Explain any behavioral steps or skills which may need to be altered or added for those people, areas, and/or situations.
- Divide the class into small discussion groups and give them the following prompt:
  - *How can you join a conversation in a respectful way?*

Contributing to a Discussion (Joining in a Conversation)

THURSDAY	■ Review the steps of the skill as well as the reasons for using it. ■ Ask students to share examples of how they have used the skill at home or with other adults/peers. ■ Identify people, areas, and/or situations (store, restaurant, public event, etc.) where students might use the skill in their community. ■ Explain any behavioral steps or skills which may need to be altered or added for those people, areas, and/or situations. ▶ Watch a video, such as *A Simple Game to Never Run Out of Things to Say in Conversation** (4:17): https://www.youtube.com/watch?v=QXiAPiw7vfc. **Note: The word "sucks" is used visually and audibly around the 15-second mark, and may not be suitable for your audience.* ■ Divide the class into small discussion groups and give them the following prompt: • *When is the best time to contribute to a discussion?*
FRIDAY	■ Review the steps of the skill as well as the reasons for using it. ■ Ask students to share examples of how they have used the skill in their community. ■ Engage students in discussions about how the skill of **Contributing to a Discussion (Joining in a Conversation)** has helped them, or in what situations it was difficult. ■ Encourage students to think about how the skill might be used in a future job/career, hobby, or other area of interest.

Contributing to a Discussion (Joining in a Conversation)

1. Approach the group (or people in conversation) quietly.

2. Look at the person speaking and listen to what is being talked about.

3. Keep a relaxed, attentive posture and nod your head to show interest.

4. Wait for a pause before making any comments.

5. Share something related to the topic, without exaggerating or dominating the conversation.

Self-Reporting Your Own Behaviors/ Communicating Honestly

SUGGESTED MATERIALS	■ *Well, I Can Top That!* by Julia Cook ■ *Cheaters Never Prosper* by Julia Cook ■ *The "I" in Integrity* by Julia Cook ■ *Responsible ME! Teacher Activity Guide* by Julia Cook ■ *Isaac the Instigator* by Jeff Tucker
LESSON OBJECTIVES	■ Recognize how to self-report their own behaviors in a variety of situations and settings. ■ Determine what the skill of **Self-Reporting Your Own Behaviors** looks and sounds like in their classroom. ■ Demonstrate the skill of **Self-Reporting Your Own Behaviors** in school, at home, and in other environments. ■ Review prior knowledge of **Self-Reporting Your Own Behaviors** within the school environment. ■ Analyze community-based situations to identify where, when, and with whom the skill of **Self-Reporting Your Own Behaviors** may be used. ■ Evaluate how the skill of **Self-Reporting Your Own Behaviors** might apply to various jobs or areas of interest.
ESSENTIAL QUESTIONS	✔ *What does self-reporting your behaviors sound and look like?* ✔ *How do you know when you need to self-report your behaviors?* ✔ *How can you self-report your behaviors in a respectful way?* ✔ *What are some words you can say to show manners and respect when self-reporting your behaviors?* ✔ *When is the best time to self-report your behaviors?* ✔ *When self-reporting your behaviors, how do you expect others to respond? Are your expectations reasonable, or do they need adjusting?*

★ SKILL STEPS

Self-Reporting Your Own Behaviors

1. Identify the behavior you feel needs to be reported.
2. Look at the person.
3. Remain calm and use a neutral voice.
4. Describe the behaviors you are reporting honestly and avoid making excuses.
5. Respond to any questions without hesitating.
6. Include others in your report if needed.

→

REASONS

- *Makes others see you as honest and mature.*
- *Shows respect for others.*
- *Keeps you and others safe.*

+ SKILL EXTENSION:

Communicating Honestly

Self-Reporting Your Own Behaviors/ Communicating Honestly

LESSON ACTIVITIES AND ASSESSMENTS	■ Role-play scenarios (see appendix) that allow students to practice the skill of **Self-Reporting Your Own Behaviors** while using different tones of voice (mad, sad, loud, calm, respectful, etc.). ■ Instruct students to write in their *SEL Journals* about how they use both skills and what specific words they say when communicating honestly and self-reporting their own behaviors. ■ Provide students an opportunity to teach the skills to their peers from other classes or students from a lower grade. ■ Use the think-pair-share technique. Have students partner up to discuss or role-play how to self-report their own behaviors using the following prompt: *How do you know when you should self-report your own behaviors?* ■ Instruct students to write about or draw in their *SEL Journals* a situation where they did not communicate honestly or self-report their behaviors. Ask for volunteers to share their experiences with the class, if appropriate.

Self-Reporting Your Own Behaviors/Communicating Honestly

MONDAY	■ Have students identify when it is okay to self-report their own behaviors in various school situations or settings (playground, cafeteria, library/media center, health office, counseling office, with a substitute teacher, etc.). ■ State the name of the skill, its behavioral steps, and reasons to use the skill. ■ Model or demonstrate the skill. ■ Read *Cheaters Never Prosper* or *Well, I Can Top That!* by Julia Cook, then lead a class discussion about what students learned from the story.
TUESDAY	■ Review the steps of the skill as well as the reasons for using it. ■ Identify people, areas, and/or situations where students might use the skill at school (playground, cafeteria, library/media center, health office, counseling office, with a substitute teacher, etc.). ■ Explain any behavioral steps or skills which may need to be altered or added for those people, areas, and/or situations. ■ Share examples you've witnessed in your classroom of students using the skill. ■ Use the think-pair-share technique. Have students partner up to discuss or role-play the skill using the following prompt: *Why is it important to know how to self-report your own behaviors?*
WEDNESDAY	■ Review the steps of the skill as well as the reasons for using it. ■ Share examples you've witnessed around school of students using the skill. ■ Identify people, areas, and/or situations where students might use the skill at home or with other significant adults or peers (teammates, neighborhood friends, family members/caregivers, etc.). ■ Explain any behavioral steps or skills which may need to be altered or added for those people, areas, and/or situations. ✚ Extend the learning by introducing the skill of **Communicating Honestly** and its behavioral steps. Explain how this skill complements the skill of **Self-Reporting Your Own Behaviors** and how both skills can be used in school, at home, and in the community. **Communicating Honestly** skill steps: 1. Look at the person. 2. Use a clear voice and avoid hesitating. 3. Share information, including all important facts and details. 4. Respond calmly to any questions. 5. Take responsibility for your behavior.

Self-Reporting Your Own Behaviors/Communicating Honestly

THURSDAY	■ Review the steps of both skills as well as the reasons for using them. ■ Ask students to share examples of how they have used the skills at home or with other adults/peers. ■ Identify people, areas, and/or situations (store, restaurant, public event, etc.) where students might use the skills in their community. ■ Explain any behavioral steps or skills which may need to be altered or added for those people, areas, and/or situations. ■ Invite students to practice the skills with a partner using a role-play scenario they create or one you provide (see appendix). ■ Read *Isaac the Instigator* by Jeff Tucker, then lead a class discussion using the following prompt: *What does Isaac's behavior teach us about the importance of communicating honestly with others?*
FRIDAY	■ Review the steps of both skills as well as the reasons for using them. ■ Ask students to share examples of how they have used either skill in their community. ■ Engage students in discussions about how the skill of **Self-Reporting Your Own Behaviors** and the skill of **Communicating Honestly** have helped them, or in what situations it was difficult. ■ Encourage students to think about how both skills might be used in a future job/career, hobby, or other area of interest. ■ Read *The "I" in Integrity* by Julia Cook, then lead a class discussion about what lessons students learned from Cora June.

Self-Reporting Your Own Behaviors

1. Identify the behavior you feel needs to be reported.

2. Look at the person.

3. Remain calm and use a neutral voice.

4. Describe the behaviors you are reporting honestly and avoid making excuses.

5. Respond to any questions without hesitating.

6. Include others in your report if needed.

Communicating Honestly

1. **Look at the person.**

2. **Use a clear voice and avoid hesitating.**

3. **Share information, including all important facts and details.**

4. **Respond calmly to any questions.**

5. **Take responsibility for your behavior.**

Waiting Your Turn

SUGGESTED MATERIALS	■ *Practicing Patience* and *Practicing Patience Downloadable Activities* by Jennifer Law ■ *Awesome Dawson It's NOT Your Turn!* by Julia Cook
LESSON OBJECTIVES	■ Recognize how to use the skill of **Waiting Your Turn** in a variety of situations and settings. ■ Determine what the skill of **Waiting Your Turn** looks and sounds like in the classroom. ■ Demonstrate the skill of **Waiting Your Turn** in school, at home, and in other environments. ■ Explore prior knowledge of the skill within the school environment. ■ Analyze community-based situations to identify where, when, and with whom the skill may be used. ■ Evaluate how the skill of **Waiting Your Turn** might apply to various jobs or areas of interest.
ESSENTIAL QUESTIONS	✔ *What does waiting your turn sound and look like?* ✔ *Why is it important to wait your turn? How can you wait your turn in a respectful way?* ✔ *What do you do when others don't wait their turn?* ✔ *When waiting for your turn, how do you expect others to respond? Are your expectations reasonable, or do they need adjusting?*

★ SKILL STEPS

Waiting Your Turn

1. Sit or stand quietly.
2. Keep your body still.
3. Stay calm (avoid sighing, whining, or begging).
4. Participate in the activity when invited.
5. Thank the person who gives you a turn.

→

REASONS

- *People will be more likely to wait their turn if you wait for yours.*
- *Less likely to hurt someone's feelings/ make someone upset.*
- *Shows self-control and patience.*

Waiting Your Turn

LESSON ACTIVITIES AND ASSESSMENTS	■ Role-play scenarios (see appendix) that allow students to practice the skill of **Waiting Your Turn.** ■ Instruct students to write in their *SEL Journals* about how they use the skill, including the specific words/behaviors they say/do when waiting their turn. Then have them write a paragraph or draw a comic strip about a time when they didn't wait their turn in an appropriate way. ■ Provide students an opportunity to teach the skill to their peers from other classes or students from a lower grade.

Waiting Your Turn

MONDAY	■ Ask students questions to assess their background knowledge and prior experiences using the skill. ■ Have students identify when it is important to wait their turn in various environments. ■ State the name of the skill, its behavioral steps, and reasons to use the skill. ■ Model or demonstrate the skill. ■ Read *Practicing Patience* by Jennifer Law, then lead a class discussion about what students learned from the story. ■ Assign additional activities to support skill development: DOWNLOADABLE ACTIVITY: *Practicing Patience* by Jennifer Law.
TUESDAY	■ Review the steps of the skill as well as the reasons for using it. ■ Read *Awesome Dawson It's NOT Your Turn!* by Julia Cook. Then lead a class discussion about what students learned from the story. ■ Use the think-pair-share technique. Have students partner up to discuss or role-play the following prompt: *Why is it important to wait your turn?* ■ Share examples you've witnessed in your classroom of students using the skill. ■ Identify people, areas, and/or situations where students might use the skill at school (playground, cafeteria, library/media center, health office, counseling office, with a substitute teacher, etc.). ■ Explain any behavioral steps or skills which may need to be altered or added for those people, areas, and/or situations. ■ Ask students to make an entry in their *SEL Journals* describing their use of the skill and what specific words/behaviors they say/do when waiting their turn.
WEDNESDAY	■ Review the steps of the skill as well as the reasons for using it. ■ Share examples you've witnessed around school of students using the skill. ■ Identify people, areas, and/or situations where students might use the skill at home or with other significant adults or peers (teammates, neighborhood friends, family members/caregivers, etc.). ■ Explain any behavioral steps or skills which may need to be altered or added for those people, areas, and/or situations. ■ Divide the class into small discussion groups and give them the following prompt: *How can you wait your turn in a respectful way?*
THURSDAY	■ Review the steps of the skill as well as the reasons for using it. ■ Ask students to share examples of how they have used the skill at home. ■ Identify people, areas, and/or situations (store, restaurant, public event, etc.) where students might use the skill in their community. ■ Explain any behavioral steps or skills which may need to be altered or added for those areas and/or situations. ■ Invite students to practice the skill with a partner using a role-play scenario they create or one you provide (see appendix).

Waiting Your Turn

FRIDAY	■ Review the steps of the skill as well as the reasons for using it. ■ Ask students to share examples of how they have used the skill at home. ■ Provide students with an opportunity to teach the skill to their peers from other classes or students from a lower grade. ■ Use the think-pair-share technique. Have students partner up to discuss or role-play the following prompt: *How do you know when you should wait your turn?* ■ Do a group activity, such as Koosh Ball Group Story. Provide students with a prompt or partial phrase and then have them take turns adding a few words to build a story. For example, you can start with the line, "One time this old toad…." The student holding the Koosh ball (or a similar soft ball) then completes the phrase by saying up to three words. Students who want to go next, or take a turn, should raise their hand, wait until the ball is handed to them, thank the person who handed them the ball, and then say their words. This also can be a listening activity by having the participants repeat everything that was said prior to their turn.

Waiting Your Turn

1. Sit or stand quietly.

2. Keep your body still.

3. Stay calm (avoid sighing, whining, or begging).

4. Participate in the activity when invited.

5. Thank the person who gives you a turn.

BOYS TOWN.

Choosing Appropriate Words/ Using Appropriate Language

SUGGESTED MATERIALS	■ *I Can't Believe You Said That!* by Julia Cook
LESSON OBJECTIVES	■ Recognize how to choose appropriate words/use appropriate language in a variety of situations and settings. ■ Determine what the skill of **Choosing Appropriate Words/Using Appropriate Language** looks and sounds like in the classroom. ■ Demonstrate the skill of **Choosing Appropriate Words/Using Appropriate Language** in school, at home, and in other environments. ■ Explore prior knowledge of the skill within the school environment. ■ Analyze community-based situations to identify where, when, and with whom the skill may be used. ■ Evaluate how the skill of **Choosing Appropriate Words/Using Appropriate Language** might apply to various jobs or areas of interest.
ESSENTIAL QUESTIONS	✔ *What does the skill of **Choosing Appropriate Words/Using Appropriate Language** sound and look like?* ✔ *How do you choose appropriate words/use appropriate language?* ✔ *Why is it important to choose appropriate words/use appropriate language?* ✔ *What are some words you can say that show manners, respect, and are appropriate to use in any setting or situation?* ✔ *How do you respond when others do not use appropriate words/language?*

★ SKILL STEPS

Choosing Appropriate Words

1. Consider where you are and who you're with.
2. Think about what you want to say and choose words that accurately reflect your thoughts or feelings.
3. Avoid terms which others may find confusing or offensive.
4. If you realize you have offended someone, apologize immediately.

REASONS

- *People will be more likely to use appropriate words when talking to you if you use kind words when talking to them.*
- *Shows maturity.*
- *Shows respect to the people you are communicating with.*

+ SKILL EXTENSION:
Using Appropriate Language

Choosing Appropriate Words/ Using Appropriate Language

<table>
<tr>
<td valign="top">LESSON ACTIVITIES AND ASSESSMENTS</td>
<td>

- Role-play scenarios (see appendix) that allow students to practice the skill of **Choosing Appropriate Words/Using Appropriate Language** while using different tones of voice (happy, sad, loud, calm, respectful, etc.).
- Instruct students to write in their *SEL Journals* about how they use the skill during the week. Then have them write a paragraph or draw a comic strip about a time when they didn't choose appropriate words or use appropriate language.
- Provide students with an opportunity to teach the skill to their peers from other classes or students from a lower grade.
- Use the think-pair-share technique. Have students partner up to discuss or role-play the following prompt: *How can you use your words for good?*

</td>
</tr>
</table>

Choosing Appropriate Words/Using Appropriate Language

MONDAY

- Invite students to practice the skill by having them identify appropriate words/language to use in a variety of settings.
- State the name of the skill, its behavioral steps, and reasons to use the skill.
- Model and demonstrate the skill.
- Read *I Can't Believe You Said That!* by Julia Cook, then lead a class discussion about what students learned from the story.

TUESDAY

- Review the steps of the skill as well as the reasons for using it.
- ▶ Watch a video, such as *Choosing Appropriate Words* (5:30): https://www.youtube.com/watch?v=u-s9-hN4Hns.
- Share examples you've witnessed in your classroom of students using the skill.
- Identify people, areas, and/or situations where students might use the skill at school (playground, cafeteria, library/media center, health office, counseling office, with a substitute teacher, etc.).
- Explain any behavioral steps or skills which may need to be altered or added for those people, areas, and/or situations.
- Use the think-pair-share technique. Have students partner up to discuss or role-play the following prompt: *Why is it important to use appropriate words?*
- Instruct students to write in their *SEL Journals* about how they use the skill throughout the week.

WEDNESDAY

- Review the steps of the skill as well as the reasons for using it.
- Share examples you've witnessed of students using the skill around school.
- Identify people, areas, and/or situations where students might use the skill at home or with other significant adults or peers (teammates, neighborhood friends, family members/caregivers, etc.).
- Explain any behavioral steps or skills which may need to be altered or added for those people, areas, and/or situations.
- ✚ Extend the learning by introducing the skill of **Using Appropriate Language** and its skill steps.

Using Appropriate Language skill steps:
1. Choose words that accurately reflect your thoughts and feelings.
2. Avoid making blaming statements.
3. Know the meaning of words and phrases you choose.
4. Avoid profanity, slang, or terms others may find offensive.
5. Frequently ask if you are being clear and understood.

- Discuss how both skills complement each other.
- Divide the class into small discussion groups and give them the following prompt: *How do you respond when others do not use appropriate words/language?*

Choosing Appropriate Words/Using Appropriate Language

THURSDAY	■ Review the steps of the skills as well as the reasons for using them.
	■ Ask students to share examples of how they have used the skills at home.
	■ Invite students to practice the skills with a partner using a role-play scenario they create or one you provide (see appendix).
	■ Instruct students to write in their *SEL Journals* an answer to the following question: *How do your words have power?*
	▶ Watch a video, such as *Power of Positive Words* (2:24): https://www.youtube.com/watch?v=I87tt00sMkM.
	  • *Point out how the students' faces lit up when they saw the kind words written about them. Remind students that their words have power and encourage them to use their words for good.*
	  • *Do a similar activity in your classroom, if appropriate. You can choose one student each day to highlight. Take a photo of each student's board to capture the words written about them and/or to create an end-of-year slideshow.*

FRIDAY	■ Review the steps of the skills as well as the reasons for using them. ■ Ask students to share examples of how they have used the skills in their community. ■ Have students write in their *SEL Journals* about how the skill of **Choosing Appropriate Words/Using Appropriate Language** might be used in a future job/career or other settings.

Choosing Appropriate Words

1. Consider where you are and who you're with.

2. Think about what you want to say and choose words that accurately reflect your thoughts or feelings.

3. Avoid terms which others may find confusing or offensive.

4. If you realize you have offended someone, apologize immediately.

Using Appropriate Language

1. Choose words that accurately reflect your thoughts and feelings.

2. Avoid making blaming statements.

3. Know the meaning of words and phrases you choose.

4. Avoid profanity, slang, or terms others may find offensive.

5. Frequently ask if you are being clear and understood.

Asking for Time to Cool Down

SUGGESTED MATERIALS	■ *Pause Power* and *Pause Power Downloadable Activities* by Jennifer Law ■ *Awesome Dawson Has Big Emotions* by Julia Cook ■ *My Day Is Ruined!* and *My Day Is Ruined! Downloadable Activities* by Bryan Smith
LESSON OBJECTIVES	■ Recognize how to use the skill of **Asking for Time to Cool Down** in a variety of situations and settings. ■ Determine what the skill of **Asking for Time to Cool Down** looks and sounds like. ■ Demonstrate the skill of **Asking for Time to Cool Down** in school, at home, and in other environments. ■ Explore prior knowledge of the skill within the school environment. ■ Analyze community-based situations to identify where, when, and with whom the skill may be used. ■ Evaluate how the skill of **Asking for Time to Cool Down** might apply to various jobs or areas of interest.
ESSENTIAL QUESTIONS	✔ *What does the skill of **Asking for Time to Cool Down** look and sound like?* ✔ *How do you know when you need to ask someone for time to cool down?* ✔ *How can you ask for time to cool down in a respectful way?* ✔ *What are some words you can say to show manners and respect when you ask for time to cool down?* ✔ *When is the best time to ask for time to cool down?* ✔ *When asking for time to cool down, how do you expect others to respond? Are your expectations reasonable, or do they need adjusting?*

★ SKILL STEPS		REASONS
Asking for Time to Cool Down 1. Recognize when you are getting frustrated. 2. Calmly get the attention of an adult. 3. Use a quiet voice and ask, "Can I please have a few minutes to calm down?" 4. If the answer is "Yes," use the provided time to practice your relaxation strategies. 5. If the answer is "No," accept the no answer and try to remain calm.	→	• *More likely to be able to control your emotions.* • *Less likely to make bad decisions and get in trouble.* • *More likely to make good decisions.* • *More apt to keep yourself and others around you safe.*

Asking for Time to Cool Down

<table>
<tr>
<td>LESSON ACTIVITIES AND ASSESSMENTS</td>
<td>

- Role-play scenarios that allow students to practice the skill of **Asking for Time to Cool Down** while using different tones of voice.
- Instruct students to write in their *SEL Journals* about how they use the skill, including the specific words they say when respectfully asking for time to cool down. Then have them write a paragraph or draw a comic strip about a situation where they did not ask for time to cool down. Ask for volunteers to share their examples, if appropriate.
- Provide students with an opportunity to teach the skill to their peers from other classes or students from a lower grade.
- Use the think-pair-share technique. Have students partner up to discuss or role-play the skill of **Asking for Time to Cool Down** using the following prompt: *How do you know when you should ask someone for time to cool down?*

</td>
</tr>
</table>

Asking for Time to Cool Down

MONDAY	■ Invite students to practice the skill by having them identify situations where it is important to ask for time to cool down when they are in various environments. ■ State the name of the skill, its behavioral steps, and reasons to use the skill. ■ Model or demonstrate the skill. ■ Read *Pause Power,* then assign additional activities to support skill development: DOWNLOADABLE ACTIVITIES: *Pause Power* by Jennifer Law. ■ Have students practice the skill by doing the following role-play scenario: *You lost a game of kickball.*
TUESDAY	■ Review the steps of the skill as well as the reasons for using it. ▶ Watch a video, such as *Story Time with Lynn: A Little Peaceful Spot by Diane Alber* (5:54): https://www.youtube.com/watch?v=0hnRCjjyhyo. ▶ Use the think-pair-share technique. Have students partner up to discuss or role-play the following prompt: *What are things that help calm you and make you feel more peaceful?* ■ Share examples you've witnessed in your classroom of students using the skill. ■ Identify people, areas, and/or situations where students might use the skill at school (playground, cafeteria, library/media center, health office, counseling office, with a substitute teacher, etc.). ■ Explain any behavioral steps or skills which may need to be altered or added for those people, areas, and/or situations. ■ Instruct students to write in their *SEL Journals.* Have them describe their use of the skill and what specific words they say when respectfully asking for time to cool down.
WEDNESDAY	■ Review the steps of the skill as well as the reasons for using it. ■ Share examples you've witnessed around school of students using the skill. ■ Identify people, areas, and/or situations where students might use the skill at home or with other significant adults or peers (teammates, neighborhood friends, family members/caregivers, etc.). ■ Explain any behavioral steps or skills which may need to be altered or added for those people, areas, and/or situations. ■ Do a small-group activity, such as making Brain Break cards. Design and create Brain Break cards students can use when they need to regulate and calm their emotions. Have students role-play and practice asking permission using their cards. • *Note: Before doing the activity, view the following video for suggestions on creating a calm down center and the steps and procedures students can follow when using their Brain Break cards.* https://www.youtube.com/watch?v=DQbuu5ufHyA (5:49).

Asking for Time to Cool Down

THURSDAY	■ Review the steps of the skill as well as the reasons for using it. ■ Ask students to share examples of how they have used the skill at home. ■ Have students write in their *SEL Journals* answers to the following questions: *When you are asking for time to cool down, how do you expect others to respond?* *Are your expectations reasonable, or do they need adjusting?* ■ Read ***Awesome Dawson Has Big Emotions*** by Julia Cook, then lead a group discussion about what students learned from the story. ■ Have students practice the skill by doing a role-play scenario they create or one you provide (see appendix).
FRIDAY	■ Review the steps of the skill as well as the reasons for using it. ■ Ask students to share examples of how they have used the skill in their community. ■ Read ***My Day Is Ruined!***, then assign additional activities to support skill development: DOWNLOADABLE ACTIVITIES: ***My Day Is Ruined!*** by Bryan Smith. ■ Engage students in discussions about how using the skill has helped them, or in what situations it was difficult. ■ Encourage students to think about how the skill might be used in a future job/career, hobby, or other area of interest.

Asking for Time to Cool Down

1. Recognize when you are getting frustrated.

2. Calmly get the attention of an adult.

3. Use a quiet voice and ask, "Can I please have a few minutes to calm down?"

4. If the answer is "Yes," use the provided time to practice your relaxation strategies.

5. If the answer is "No," accept the no answer and try to remain calm.

Using Structured Problem-Solving (SODAS)

SUGGESTED MATERIALS	■ *What's the Problem?* and *What's the Problem? Downloadable Activities* by Bryan Smith
LESSON OBJECTIVES	■ Recognize how to use the skill of **Using Structured Problem-Solving** in a variety of situations and settings. ■ Determine what structured problem-solving looks and sounds like in the classroom. ■ Demonstrate the skill of **Using Structured Problem-Solving** in school, at home, and in other environments. ■ Explore prior knowledge of the skill within the school environment. ■ Analyze community-based situations to identify where, when, and with whom the skill of **Using Structured Problem-Solving** may be used. ■ Evaluate how the skill of **Using Structured Problem-Solving** might apply to various jobs or areas of interest.
ESSENTIAL QUESTIONS	✔ *What does structured problem-solving sound and look like?* ✔ *How do you know when you need to use structured problem-solving? How can you use structured problem-solving in a respectful way?* ✔ *What are some words you can say to show manners and respect when you use structured problem-solving?* ✔ *When is the best time to use structured problem-solving?* ✔ *When using structured problem-solving, how do you expect others to respond? Are your expectations reasonable, or do they need adjusting?*

★ SKILL STEPS

Using Structured Problem-Solving (SODAS)

1. Define the problem **S**ituation.
2. Generate two or more **O**ptions.
3. Look at each option's potential **D**isadvantages.
4. Look at each option's potential **A**dvantages.
5. Decide on the best **S**olution.

→

REASONS

- *Helps you think about the possible outcomes of your choices.*
- *Allows you to find the disadvantages and advantages of choosing different behaviors.*
- *Helps you focus on what you can do to make things better rather than worse.*
- *More likely to make good decisions.*

Using Structured Problem-Solving (SODAS)

LESSON ACTIVITIES AND ASSESSMENTS	■ Role-play scenarios (see appendix) that allow students to practice the skill of **Using Structured Problem-Solving (SODAS)**. ■ Instruct students to write in their *SEL Journals* about how they use the skill, including what specific words they say or actions they take when problem-solving. Then have them write a paragraph or draw a comic strip about a time when they did not problem-solve successfully or in an appropriate way. ■ Provide students with an opportunity to teach the skill to their peers from other classes or students from a lower grade. ■ Use the think-pair-share technique. Have students partner up to discuss or role-play the skill using the following prompt: *How do you know when you should use structured problem-solving?*

Using Structured Problem-Solving (SODAS)

MONDAY	■ Invite students to practice the skill by having them identify situations where structured problem-solving would help them. ■ State the name of the skill, its behavioral steps, and the reasons for using the skill. ■ Model or demonstrate the skill. ■ Invite students to practice the skill independently or with others using a role-play scenario (see appendix).
TUESDAY	■ Review the steps of the skill as well as the reasons for using it. ■ Read *What's the Problem?*, then assign additional activities to support skill development: DOWNLOADABLE ACTIVITIES: *What's the Problem?* by Bryan Smith. ■ Share examples you've witnessed in the classroom of students using the skill. ■ Identify people, areas, and/or situations where students might use the skill at school (playground, cafeteria, library/media center, health office, counseling office, with a substitute teacher, etc.). ■ Explain any behavioral steps or skills which may need to be altered or added for those people, areas, and/or situations. ■ Instruct students to write in their *SEL Journals.* Have them describe their use of the skill and what specific words they say or actions they take when problem-solving.
WEDNESDAY	■ Review the steps of the skill as well as the reasons for using it. ■ Share examples you've witnessed around school of students using the skill. ■ Identify people, areas, and/or situations where students might use the skill at home or with other significant adults or peers (teammates, neighborhood friends, family members/caregivers, etc.). ■ Explain any behavioral steps or skills which may need to be altered or added for those situations or locations. ■ Divide the class into small discussion groups and give them the following prompt: *How can you use structured problem-solving in a respectful way?*
THURSDAY	■ Review the steps of the skill as well as the reasons for using it. ■ Identify people, areas, and/or situations (store, restaurant, public event, etc.) where students might use the skill in their community. ■ Explain any behavioral steps or skills which may need to be altered or added for those people, areas, and/or situations. ■ Group students in pairs and have them discuss the following question: *When is the best time to use structured problem-solving?*

Using Structured Problem-Solving (SODAS)

FRIDAY	■ Review the steps of the skill as well as the reasons for using it. ■ Ask students to share examples of how they have used the skill in their community. ■ Engage students in discussions about how using the skill has helped them, or in what situations it was difficult. ■ Encourage students to think about how the skill might be used in a future job/career, hobby, or other area of interest. ■ Do a group activity, such as Sticky Situations. Have students practice using structured problem-solving in the following situations: • *You notice several older students making fun of a younger student on the playground. You don't know if you should tell the older students to stop, or if you should go tell an adult, or if you should ignore the situation.* • *Your friend tells you the answer key to the upcoming quiz is on the teacher's desk. You need to get a good grade on the quiz, and you're tempted to go up to the desk while the teacher is distracted and take a peek at the answers.* • *You are going to be late for class and someone is in your way, preventing you from getting to your locker.* • *Coach tells you someone else is going to start in your place for today's soccer game.*

Using Structured Problem-Solving (SODAS)

1. Define the problem **S**ituation.

2. Generate two or more **O**ptions.

3. Look at each option's potential **D**isadvantages.

4. Look at each option's potential **A**dvantages.

5. Decide on the best **S**olution.

Reporting Other Youths' Behavior (Peer Reporting)

SUGGESTED MATERIALS	■ *My Name's Sammy, and I'm No Snitch* and *My Name's Sammy, and I'm No Snitch Downloadable Activities* by Jeff Tucker ■ *Diamond Rattle Loves to Tattle* and *Diamond Rattle Loves to Tattle Downloadable Activities* by Ashley Bartley
LESSON OBJECTIVES	■ Recognize how to report other youths' behavior in a variety of situations and settings. ■ Determine what the skill of **Reporting Other Youths' Behavior (Peer Reporting)** looks and sounds like in their classroom. ■ Demonstrate the skill of **Reporting Other Youths' Behavior (Peer Reporting)** in school, at home, and in other environments. ■ Explore prior knowledge of the skill within the school environment. ■ Analyze community-based situations to identify where, when, and with whom the skill of **Reporting Other Youths' Behavior (Peer Reporting)** may be used. ■ Evaluate how the skill of **Reporting Other Youths' Behavior (Peer Reporting)** might apply to various jobs or areas of interest.
ESSENTIAL QUESTIONS	✔ *What does the skill of **Reporting Other Youths' Behavior (Peer Reporting)** look and sound like?* ✔ *How do you know when you need to report the behaviors of others?* ✔ *How can you report the behaviors of others in a respectful way?* ✔ *What are some words you can say to show manners and respect when reporting the behaviors of others? When is the best time to report the behaviors of others?* ✔ *When you report other youths' behavior, how do you expect them to respond? Are your expectations reasonable, or do they need adjusting?*

★ SKILL STEPS

Reporting Other Youths' Behavior (Peer Reporting)

1. Identify a trusted adult.
2. Look at the person.
3. Use a clear, concerned voice.
4. Describe specifically the inappropriate behavior you are reporting.
5. Give a reason for the report that shows concern.
6. Answer any questions truthfully and be prepared to provide details.

→

REASONS

- *Helps keep you and your peers safe.*
- *Shows responsibility.*
- *More likely to get into trouble if you see dangerous behavior and do not report it.*

Reporting Other Youths' Behavior (Peer Reporting)

<table>
<tr><td>LESSON ACTIVITIES AND ASSESSMENTS</td><td>

- Role-play scenarios that allow students to practice the skill of **Reporting Other Youths' Behavior (Peer Reporting)** while using different tones of voice (mad, sad, loud, calm, respectful, etc.).
- Instruct students to write in their *SEL Journals* about how they use the skill, including what specific words they say or actions they take when peer reporting.
- Provide students with an opportunity to teach the skill to their peers from other classes or students from a lower grade.
- Use the think-pair-share technique. Have students partner up to create role-plays where they use the skill of **Reporting Other Youths' Behavior (Peer Reporting)**.

</td></tr>
</table>

Reporting Other Youths' Behavior (Peer Reporting)

<table>
<tr><td>MONDAY</td><td>

- Invite students to practice the skill by having them identify when they should report the behaviors of others.
- State the name of the skill, its behavioral steps, and the reasons for using the skill.
- Model and demonstrate the skill.
- Read *My Name's Sammy, and I'm No Snitch* by Jeff Tucker.
- Assign additional activities to support skill development: DOWNLOADABLE ACTIVITY: *My Name's Sammy, and I'm No Snitch* (Grades K-3); *My Name's Sammy, and I'm No Snitch* (Grades 4-6) by Jeff Tucker.

</td></tr>
<tr><td>TUESDAY</td><td>

- Review the steps of the skill as well as the reasons for using it.
- Share examples you've witnessed in your classroom of students using the skill.
- Identify people, areas, and/or situations where students might use the skill at school (playground, cafeteria, library/media center, health office, counseling office, with a substitute teacher, etc.).
- Explain any behavioral steps or skills which may need to be altered or added for those people, areas, and/or situations.
- Instruct students to write in their *SEL Journals*. Have them describe their use of the skill and what specific words they might say when peer reporting.

</td></tr>
<tr><td>WEDNESDAY</td><td>

- Review the steps of the skill as well as the reasons for using it.
- Share examples you've witnessed around school of students using the skill.
- Identify people, areas, and/or situations where students might use the skill at home or with other adults or peers (teammates, neighborhood friends, family members/caregivers, etc.).
- Explain any behavioral steps or skills which may need to be altered or added for those people, areas, and/or situations.
- Divide the class into small discussion groups and give them the following prompt: *What is the difference between telling and tattling?*

</td></tr>
<tr><td>THURSDAY</td><td>

- Review the steps of the skill as well as the reasons for using it.
- Ask students to share examples of how they have used the skill at home.
- Identify people, areas, and/or situations (store, restaurant, public event, etc.) where students might use the skill in their community.
- Explain any behavioral steps or skills which may need to be altered or added for those areas or situations.
- Read *Diamond Rattle Loves to Tattle*, then assign additional activities to support skill development: DOWNLOADABLE ACTIVITIES: *Diamond Rattle Loves to Tattle* by Ashley Bartley.
- Have students practice the skill by doing one or more role-play scenarios (see appendix).

</td></tr>
</table>

Reporting Other Youths' Behavior (Peer Reporting)

FRIDAY	■ Review the steps of the skill as well as the reasons for using it. ■ Ask students to share examples of how they have used the skill in their community. ■ Engage students in discussions about how using the skill has helped them, or in what situations it was difficult. ■ Invite students to think about how the skill might be used in a future job, hobby, or other area of interest.

Reporting Other Youths' Behavior (Peer Reporting)

1. Identify a trusted adult.

2. Look at the person.

3. Use a clear, concerned voice.

4. Describe specifically the inappropriate behavior you are reporting.

5. Give a reason for the report that shows concern.

6. Answer any questions truthfully and be prepared to provide details.

BOYS TOWN.

Caring for the Property of Others

SUGGESTED MATERIALS	■ *But It's Not My Fault* by Julia Cook ■ *Respect and Take Care of Things* by Cheri J. Meiners
LESSON OBJECTIVES	■ Recognize how to use the skill of **Caring for the Property of Others** in a variety of situations and settings. ■ Demonstrate the skill of **Caring for the Property of Others** in school, at home, and in other environments. ■ Explore prior knowledge of the skill within the school environment. ■ Analyze community-based situations to identify where, when, and with whom the skill of **Caring for the Property of Others** may be used. ■ Evaluate how the skill of **Caring for the Property of Others** might apply to various jobs or areas of interest.
ESSENTIAL QUESTIONS	✔ What does the skill of **Caring for the Property of Others** sound and look like? ✔ How do you know when you need to care for the property of others? ✔ How can you care for other people's property in a respectful way? ✔ What are some words you can say to show manners and respect when you are caring for others' property? ✔ What are some of the best ways and times to care for the property of others? ✔ When you care for the property of others, how do you expect others to respond? Are your expectations reasonable, or do they need adjusting?

★ SKILL STEPS

Caring for the Property of Others

1. Before using something belonging to another person, ask their permission.

2. Use the item as it is supposed to be used or according to the instructions.

3. Take care of the property as if it were your own.

4. If something gets broken, apologize and offer to repair or replace it.

→

REASONS

- *People are more likely to trust you to look after/borrow their things.*

- *Shows others you are respectful and responsible.*

Caring for the Property of Others

<table>
<tr>
<td>LESSON ACTIVITIES AND ASSESSMENTS</td>
<td>

■ Lead a class discussion using the following prompts:

- *Why is it important to respect your own property? Do you think you take better care of things that you purchased with your own money? If you could only carry three things out of your burning home, what would you take? How would you feel if someone broke one of those things?*

■ Instruct students to write in their *SEL Journals* about how they use the skill, including the specific words they say and actions they take when caring for the property of others. Then have them write a paragraph or draw a comic strip about a situation where they did not care for someone's property in a respectful way.

■ Provide students with an opportunity to teach the skill to their peers from other classes or students from a lower grade.

■ Use the think-pair-share technique. Have students partner up to discuss or role-play the skill using the following prompt: *How can you care for the property of others in a respectful way?*

</td>
</tr>
</table>

Caring for the Property of Others

MONDAY	■ Invite students to practice the skill by having them identify how to care for the property of others in various school environments. ■ State the name of the skill, its behavioral steps, and reasons to use the skill. ■ Model and demonstrate the skill. ■ Have students practice the skill by doing one or more role-play scenarios (see appendix).
TUESDAY	■ Review the steps of the skill as well as the reasons for using it. ■ Use the think-pair-share technique. Have students partner up to discuss or role-play the skill using the following prompt: *Why is it important to respect property?* ■ Share examples you've witnessed in your classroom of students using the skill. ■ Identify people, areas, and/or situations where students might use the skill at school (playground, cafeteria, library/media center, health office, counseling office, with a substitute teacher, etc.). ■ Explain any behavioral steps or skills which may need to be altered or added for those people, areas, and/or situations. ■ Instruct students to write in their *SEL Journals*. Have them describe their use of the skill and what specific words they say and actions they take when they care for the property of others.
WEDNESDAY	■ Review the steps of the skill as well as the reasons for using it. ■ Share examples you've witnessed around school of students using the skill. ■ Read ***Respect and Take Care of Things*** by Cheri J. Meiners, then lead a group discussion and ask students what they learned from reading the story. ■ Divide the class into small discussion groups and give them the following prompts: *If you could save three things from your burning home, what would you save? How would you feel if someone broke one of those things?* ■ Identify people, areas, and/or situations where students might use the skill at home or with other significant adults or peers (teammates, neighborhood friends, family members/caregivers, etc.). ■ Explain any behavioral steps or skills which may need to be altered or added for those people, areas, and/or situations.
THURSDAY	■ Review the steps of the skill as well as the reasons for using it. ■ Ask students to share examples of how they have used the skill at home or with other adults/peers. ■ Instruct students to write in their *SEL Journals*. Have them answer the following questions: *When you care for someone's property, how do you expect them to respond? Are your expectations reasonable, or do they need adjusting?* ■ Have students practice the skill by doing a role-play scenario they create or one you provide (see appendix).

Caring for the Property of Others

FRIDAY	■ Review the steps of the skill as well as the reasons for using it. ■ Ask students to share examples of how they have used the skill in their community. ■ Engage students in discussions about how using the skill has helped them, or in what situations it was difficult. ■ Ask students to write in their *SEL Journals* about how they might use the skill in a future job, hobby, or other area of interest.

Caring for the Property of Others

1. Before using something belonging to another person, ask their permission.

2. Use the item as it is supposed to be used or according to the instructions.

3. Take care of the property as if it were your own.

4. If something gets broken, apologize and offer to repair or replace it.

Making Positive Self-Statements/Interrupting or Changing Negative or Harmful Thoughts

SUGGESTED MATERIALS	■ *Is There an App for That?* and *Is There an App for That? Activity Guide* by Bryan Smith ■ *Parker Plum and the Rotten Egg Thoughts* and *Parker Plum and the Rotten Egg Thoughts Downloadable Activities* by Billie Pavicic ■ *Molly and the Runaway Trolley* and *Molly and the Runaway Trolley Downloadable Activities* by Ashley Bartley
LESSON OBJECTIVES	■ Recognize how to make positive self-statements in a variety of situations and settings. ■ Determine what the skill of **Making Positive Self-Statements** looks and sounds like in their classroom. ■ Demonstrate the skill of **Making Positive Self-Statements** in school, at home, and in other environments. ■ Explore prior knowledge of the skill within the school environment. ■ Analyze community-based situations to identify where, when, and with whom the skill of **Making Positive Self-Statements** may be used. ■ Evaluate how the skill of **Making Positive Self-Statements** might apply to various jobs or areas of interest.
ESSENTIAL QUESTIONS	✔ *What does the skill of **Making Positive Self-Statements** look and sound like?* ✔ *How do you know when you need to make positive self-statements?* ✔ *How can you make positive self-statements in a respectful way?* ✔ *What are some words you can say when you make a positive self-statement?* ✔ *When is the best time to make a positive self-statement?* ✔ *Why is it important to learn how to make positive self-statements?*

★ SKILL STEPS

Making Positive Self-Statements

1. Identify the things you do well.
2. Share your accomplishments honestly and avoid exaggerating.
3. Begin by saying out loud or to yourself, "I'm proud of…" or "I think I did well at…."
4. Avoid putting down the efforts of others.

→

REASONS

- *Helps build confidence and self-esteem.*
- *Less likely to feel bad about yourself.*

＋ SKILL EXTENSION:
Interrupting or Changing Negative or Harmful Thoughts

Making Positive Self-Statements/Interrupting or Changing Negative or Harmful Thoughts

<table>
<tr>
<td>LESSON ACTIVITIES AND ASSESSMENTS</td>
<td>

- Role-play scenarios (see appendix) that allow students to practice the skill.
- Instruct students to write in their *SEL Journals* about how they use the skill, including the specific words they say when making positive self-statements. Then have them write a paragraph or draw a comic strip about a situation where they did not change their negative or harmful thoughts.
- Provide students with an opportunity to teach the skill to their peers from other classes or students from a lower grade.
- Use the think-pair-share technique. Have students partner up to discuss how to make positive self-statements using the following prompt: *What is a magic word I can say to myself to stop negative thoughts and think positively?*

</td>
</tr>
</table>

Making Positive Self-Statements/
Interrupting or Changing Negative or Harmful Thoughts

MONDAY

- Invite students to practice the skill by having them identify situations where it is helpful to make positive self-statements in various school environments.
- State the name of the skill, its behavioral steps, and reasons to use the skill.
- Model and demonstrate the skill.
- Invite students to practice the skill independently or with a partner using the following prompts:
  - *I successfully completed or achieved _____________.*
  - *I am proud of myself for _______________.*
  - *I did well at _______________.*

TUESDAY

- Review the steps of the skill as well as the reasons for using it.
- Share examples you've witnessed around school of students using the skill.
- ▶ Watch a video, such as *Making Positive Self Statements* (4:52): https://www.youtube.com/watch?v=tMoHBVOM6Ks.
- Use the think-pair-share technique. Have students partner up to discuss or role-play the following prompt: *Why is it important to learn to make positive self-statements?*
- Instruct students to write in their *SEL Journals*. Have them describe their use of the skill and what specific words they say when making positive self-statements.

WEDNESDAY

- Review the steps of the skill as well as the reasons for using it.
- Share examples you've witnessed in your classroom of students using the skill.
- Read *Is There an App for That?* by Bryan Smith or *Parker Plum and the Rotten Egg Thoughts* by Billie Pavicic. Assign additional activities to support skill development using the *Is There an App for That? Activity Guide* or the *Parker Plum and the Rotten Egg Thoughts Downloadable Activities*.
- ✚ Extend the learning by introducing the skill of **Interrupting or Changing Negative or Harmful Thoughts**. Explain how this skill complements the skill of **Making Positive Self-Statements** and how both skills can be used.

  Interrupting or Changing Negative or Harmful Thoughts skill steps:
  1. Identify the unpleasant or harmful thoughts you find yourself having regularly.
  2. Think about the negative consequences these thoughts can have on you or others.
  3. Instruct yourself to "stop" or tell yourself, "I'm not going to think about this anymore."
  4. Replace the negative thought with a positive, true, or logical statement or positive distraction or activity.
  5. Recognize and acknowledge your progress.
  6. If these thoughts persist, speak with a trusted adult.

Making Positive Self-Statements/
Interrupting or Changing Negative or Harmful Thoughts

THURSDAY	■ Identify people, areas, and/or situations (store, restaurant, public event, etc.) where students might use either skill in their community. ■ Explain any steps or skills which may need to be altered or added for these people, areas, and/or situations. ■ Ask students to share examples of how they have used both skills outside of school. ■ Do a group activity, such as Self-Affirmation. Have students choose a self-affirmation word or phrase that is true about themselves or that will give them confidence. Instruct them to write their affirmation on a sticky note and post it where they can see it every day. ■ Invite students to practice the skills independently or with others using role-play scenarios they create or one you provide (see appendix).
FRIDAY	■ Review the steps of the skills as well as the reasons for using them. ■ Ask students to share examples of how they have used the skills in their community. ■ Engage students in discussions about how using the skills have helped them, or in what situations it was difficult. ■ Encourage students to think about how the skills might be used in a future job/career, hobby, or other area of interest. ■ Read *Molly and the Runaway Trolley*, then assign additional activities to support skill development: DOWNLOADABLE ACTIVITIES: *Molly and the Runaway Trolley* by Ashley Bartley.

Making Positive Self-Statements

1. Identify the things you do well.

2. Share your accomplishments honestly and avoid exaggerating.

3. Begin by saying out loud or to yourself, "I'm proud of..." or "I think I did well at...."

4. Avoid putting down the efforts of others.

Interrupting or Changing Negative or Harmful Thoughts

1. Identify the unpleasant or harmful thoughts you find yourself having regularly.

2. Think about the negative consequences these thoughts can have on you or others.

3. Instruct yourself to "stop" or tell yourself, "I'm not going to think about this anymore."

4. Replace the negative thought with a positive, true, or logical statement or positive distraction or activity.

5. Recognize and acknowledge your progress.

6. If these thoughts persist, speak with a trusted adult.

BOYS TOWN

Valuing Differences

SUGGESTED MATERIALS	■ *The Judgmental Flower* by Julia Cook ■ *Diversity Is Key* and *Diversity Is Key Downloadable Activities* by Bryan Smith
LESSON OBJECTIVES	■ Recognize how to value differences in a variety of situations and settings. ■ Determine what the skill of **Valuing Differences** looks and sounds like in their classroom. ■ Demonstrate the skill of **Valuing Differences** in school, at home, and in other environments. ■ Explore prior knowledge of the skill within the school environment. ■ Analyze community-based situations to identify where, when, and with whom the skill of **Valuing Differences** may be used. ■ Evaluate how the skill of **Valuing Differences** might apply to various jobs or areas of interest.
ESSENTIAL QUESTIONS	✔ *What does the skill of **Valuing Differences** look and sound like?* ✔ *How do you know when you need to value differences?* ✔ *How can you value differences in a respectful way?* ✔ *What are some words you can say to show manners and respect when using the skill of **Valuing Differences**?* ✔ *When is the best time to value differences?* ✔ *When you value differences, how do you expect others to respond? Are your expectations reasonable, or do they need adjusting?*

★ SKILL STEPS

Valuing Differences

1. Examine the similarities between you and another person.
2. Take note of your differences.
3. Focus on the interests, traits, and activities you share.
4. Express appreciation and respect for the person as an individual.
5. Identify/demonstrate how you can learn and grow by embracing these differences.

REASONS

- *Helps people feel safe, welcome, and comfortable around you.*
- *People are more likely to accept you for who you are if you accept them for who they are.*

Valuing Differences

<table>
<tr>
<td>LESSON ACTIVITIES AND ASSESSMENTS</td>
<td>

- Role-play scenarios (see appendix) that allow students to practice the skill of **Valuing Differences** while using different tones of voice (happy, sad, loud, calm, respectful, etc.).
- Instruct students to write in their *SEL Journals* about how they use the skill, including the specific words they say or behaviors they use to show or demonstrate how they value differences. Then have them write a paragraph or draw a comic strip about a time when they did not value differences in an appropriate way.
- Provide students with an opportunity to teach the skill to their peers from other classes or students from a lower grade.
- Use the think-pair-share technique. Have students partner up to discuss or role-play how to value differences using the following prompt: *How can I value differences in a respectful way?*

</td>
</tr>
</table>

Valuing Differences

<table>
<tr><td>MONDAY</td><td>

- Invite students to practice the skill by having them determine when and why valuing differences is important in various school environments.
- State the name of the skill, its behavioral steps, and reasons to use the skill.
- Model or demonstrate the skill.
- Do a hands-on classroom activity. Have students write on a sticky note how they felt on the first day they attended a new school, or how they felt on the first day of a new school year. Ask them to compare their sticky notes with one another, then stand by those who had the same or similar feelings.

</td></tr>
<tr><td>TUESDAY</td><td>

- Review the steps of the skill as well as the reasons for using it.
- Share examples you've witnessed in your classroom of students using the skill.
- Read *The Judgmental Flower* by Julia Cook, then lead a group discussion and ask students what they learned from reading the story.
- Identify people, areas, and/or situations where students might use the skill at school (playground, cafeteria, library/media center, health office, counseling office, with a substitute teacher, etc.).
- Explain any behavioral steps or skills which may need to be altered or added for those people, areas, and/or situations.
- Instruct students to write in their *SEL Journals*. Have them describe their use of the skill and what specific words they say or behaviors they use to show or demonstrate how they value differences.

</td></tr>
<tr><td>WEDNESDAY</td><td>

- Review the steps of the skill as well as the reasons for using it.
- Share examples you've witnessed around school of students using the skill.
- Identify people, areas, and/or situations where students might use the skill at home or with other significant adults or peers (teammates, neighborhood friends, family members/caregivers, etc.).
- Explain any behavioral steps or skills which may need to be altered or added for those people, areas, and/or situations.
- Read *Diversity Is Key*, then assign additional activities to support skill development: DOWNLOADABLE ACTIVITIES: *Diversity Is Key* by Bryan Smith.

</td></tr>
</table>

Valuing Differences

THURSDAY	<ul><li>Review the steps of the skill as well as the reasons for using it.</li><li>Ask students to share examples of how they have used the skill at home or with others.</li><li>Identify people, areas, and/or situations (store, restaurant, public event, etc.) where students might use the skill in their community.</li><li>Explain any behavioral steps or skills which may need to be altered or added for those people, areas, and/or situations.</li><li>▶ Watch a video, such as *We Are All Different—and THAT'S AWESOME!* (4:39): https://www.youtube.com/watch?v=sQuM5e0QGLg.</li><li>Divide the class into small discussion groups after watching the video. Give each group the following prompts: *What are some things you noticed that were different about the young speaker, his family, and their friend Steven? Do you ever feel like you have to change or fix things that are different about you?*</li></ul>
FRIDAY	<ul><li>Review the steps of the skill as well as the reasons for using it.</li><li>Ask students to share examples of how they have used the skill in their community.</li><li>Engage students in discussions about how using the skill has helped them, or in what situations it was difficult.</li><li>Encourage students to think about how the skill might be used in a future job/career, hobby, or other area of interest.</li></ul>

Valuing Differences

1. Examine the similarities between you and another person.

2. Take note of your differences.

3. Focus on the interests, traits, and activities you share.

4. Express appreciation and respect for the person as an individual.

5. Identify/demonstrate how you can learn and grow by embracing these differences.

APPENDIX: Role-Play Scenarios

Introducing Yourself/Greeting Others

While attending a family reunion, a cousin you have never met before asks you your name and who your parents are.

A new student is sitting alone in the cafeteria. You introduce yourself and ask them if you can sit at their table. After you sit down, several of your friends join you. You greet them and introduce each of them to the new student.

You are appointed the official classroom greeter, and you have to introduce yourself and your classmates to the day's special visitors.

You are about to say hello to your former coach, but you're worried the coach won't remember you.

Following Instructions/Following Written Instructions

The teacher tells everyone to line up single file because it's time to change classrooms.

Your music teacher writes four instructions on the board and tells the class to follow them.

Your mom tells you to put your games away and come to dinner.

Your coach emails the login instructions to access the team's shared calendar.

Accepting Criticism (Feedback)/ Accepting Help or Assistance

The teacher tells you there are spelling errors and incomplete answers on your worksheet.

The teacher offers to help you correct your work.

Your older sibling says the diorama you made looks messy and weird, and then asks if you want some help.

Accepting Consequences

In the cafeteria, you and your friend are caught goofing around and are told to get out of line and sit at a table.

You kept talking to a friend sitting behind you after being told to listen and be quiet, so now you have to move to the front of the class.

Listening to Others

Your friend is telling you all about the new family pet they brought home last night.

Your little sister is telling you all about her new doll while you want to watch the movie.

Using an Appropriate Voice Tone (or Level)

After lunch, you walk into the classroom and it's very quiet. You have to ask the teacher permission to use the restroom.

Staying on Task/Ignoring Distractions

You need to complete a big assignment independently, but you're having trouble focusing because your best friends are next to you working on a group project.

As you work on your assignment, another classmate is humming and tapping their foot on the floor.

Completing a Task/Analyzing Tasks to Be Completed

Your art teacher tells the class everyone must complete their art project by the end of the class period. You are instructed to sketch your favorite animal, draw a picture that includes the animal, hang the picture in the classroom, color the picture, write a short description at the bottom of the picture, and give the picture a title. The project has many steps, and you're not sure what to do first.

The school librarian asks you to quietly put the books that are on the table back on the shelf, pick up the litter on the floor and put it in the trash can, and find a book that has a red cover.

Getting the Teacher's Attention/ Getting Another Person's Attention and Interrupting Appropriately

The gym teacher splits the class into four groups, and you don't know which group you were assigned.

Your work group has questions about the assignment. You want to ask the teacher, but he is speaking to another staff member.

Asking for Help

You and your friends are visiting an art museum and want to see a specific painting. You don't know where it is located and need to ask someone.

You're a new student and cannot remember where the science lab is located, so you ask a classmate.

Working with Others

You are partnered with two other students and have to decide who will be responsible for each of the following tasks: Researching the early life of George Washington Carver, identifying at least three of his inventions, writing a one-page report about his scientific discoveries, and making a poster with images and words highlighting his life and work.

You and a classmate you recently argued with are paired together and told to reorganize the book shelf.

Switching from One Task to Another

You are sitting at your desk reading a book when the fire alarm goes off. Your teacher tells you it's a drill and to immediately follow the classroom's fire drill procedure.

You and a friend are in the middle of watching a funny movie when your dad tells you it's time to turn off the TV and go outside.

Accepting "No" for an Answer/ Accepting Decisions of Authority

You're in a hurry and ask a stranger to let you go first in line. They say no.

You ask a friend if you can come to their brother's birthday party and are told no.

The manager of the rec center tells you and your friends to be out of the building in five minutes.

Asking for Permission/Making a Request

It's the middle of class, and you need permission to leave and go to the restroom.

You don't like your seat assignment and want to move.

A friend's coat and books are on a chair you want to sit in. You ask permission to move their stuff.

Using Anger Control (Self-Control Strategies)

A classmate makes fun of your shoes and then makes fun of your clothes.

Your project partner forgets to do a portion of the assignment, and you both lose 20 points.

Disagreeing Appropriately/ Resolving Conflicts

A classmate is bragging that their favorite professional soccer team is better than the team you like best.

Your best friend is mad at you for not helping them when they were being bullied.

You attempt to change the principal's mind after your request to bring a baby potbelly pig to school for show-and-tell is denied.

Making an Apology

You bump into someone and step on their new sneakers, which causes them to drop their lunch tray.

You lost your sibling's favorite sunglasses, and you didn't ask permission to wear them.

Offering Assistance or Help

A classmate's backpack tears open, and the contents fall all over the floor.

You see a classmate struggling to carry several large books across the room.

Your teacher is trying to rearrange desks before the start of class.

Sharing Something

A classmate asks to try some of your snack.

In art class, there is only one red marker for everyone to use.

Talking with Others (Having a Conversation)

At the science fair, you want to know more about how the color of light affects plant growth. What do you say to the student who did the project?

Your favorite team won the Super Bowl, and all your friends are talking about the game.

Accepting Compliments

A classmate tells you they like your shoes. How do you respond?

While walking your dog, a neighbor says your dog is really cute. What do you say?

Your sibling congratulates you for winning a speech contest. How do you respond?

Using Technology Appropriately (in School)

You feel your phone vibrate during a test. You're not supposed to look at or use your phone during class, but you really want to read the text message.

The school laptops block you from visiting social media sites but your friend says they figured out how to access them anyway, and they want to show you how to do it.

Asking for Clarification

You were listening to the teacher's instructions, but you think you might have forgotten one of her directions.

Your mom tells you to go help your brother clean out the garage, but then your dad tells you to go upstairs and help him clean out a closet. You don't know who you're supposed to help first, your brother or your dad.

Correcting Another Person (Giving Criticism/Feedback)

Your sibling is super proud about how well they cleaned up the kitchen after dinner. But you notice they missed a couple dirty dishes on the stove. What do you say?

A cast member in the school play is telling everyone that play practice starts at 3:30 pm, but you know it doesn't start until 4:30 pm. What do you say?

Accepting Apologies from Others

Your younger brother admits taking your skateboard without permission and apologizes.

The guidance counselor is fifteen minutes late for your scheduled meeting and apologizes.

Showing Appreciation/Giving Compliments

You show your appreciation to a classmate who let you borrow a pencil because you forgot to bring yours.

You want to compliment a student who won an academic award, but you don't know them very well.

You missed class for a couple days, so your friends share their notes with you.

Contributing to a Discussion (Joining in a Conversation)

At recess, several kids are trying to decide what game to play and who should be team captains. You try to join the discussion.

You hear two students discussing whether or not they should see the new Marvel movie. You recently saw it and are eager to share your opinion.

Two students are whispering to one another as they look at you. You want to know what they're saying or if they're talking about you.

Self-Reporting Your Own Behaviors/ Communicating Honestly

You have to explain to the teacher why you were late to class.

Your parents ask you and your sister why the carpet has a large red stain.

You saw your friend throw trash on the floor, and the teacher asks you who made the mess.

Waiting Your Turn

At the sleepover, you're next in line to use the virtual reality headset but your friend keeps playing.

After asking the teacher for a blue marker, he says you need to wait until he finishes grading a paper.

Choosing Appropriate Words/Using Appropriate Language

A friend makes a joke about you, hurting your feelings. You want to tell them the joke made you mad.

Your friend really likes their new haircut, but you hate it. Your friend asks what you think of it.

Asking for Time to Cool Down

During basketball practice, you're upset because you've missed several layups, you're getting shoved by a defender, and the coach keeps telling you to play faster.

Your group is about to give its presentation in front of the class. Two group members are arguing with you about who should speak first. A third group member tells you they didn't bring the materials you need for the presentation.

Using Structured Problem-Solving (SODAS)

You see someone cheating on an assignment.

You saw your friend bully someone on the playground.

Reporting Other Youths' Behavior (Peer Reporting)

You witnessed a student pull the fire alarm as a prank.

You saw a group of students vandalize another student's locker.

Caring for the Property of Others

You ask to borrow a math textbook. A friend agrees to let you use theirs, but only for five minutes and you're told not to mark it up or mess up any of the pages. You give the book back ten minutes later, and several pages are folded and wrinkled.

Your friend leaves class unexpectedly, and you have the rocket-shaped piggy bank they brought for show-and-tell. Your friend won't be back until tomorrow, so you have to hold onto it until they return.

Making Positive Self-Statements/ Interrupting or Changing Negative or Harmful Thoughts

You were not chosen for the lead role in the school play. You think it's because no one likes you, and your voice is too scratchy.

Your team had no turnovers during the whole game but lost anyway. What can you say to your teammates?

Valuing Differences

A new student joins the class who speaks and acts in a different way from everyone else. You respond to them in a respectful way.

A classmate has a strong opinion about a controversial issue and is always talking about it. You don't agree with them and want them to stop talking about it.

Video References

The following videos are included in one or more of the weekly lessons. At the time of publication, these videos were free and accessible without restriction. Some may have a "Subscribe Tab" or refer to supporting materials available from Teachers Pay Teachers. Video subscriptions and any of their related instructional materials were not required for our lessons. They are options offered through the video publisher.

[ABA in School]. (2022, May 6). *"I Know Voice Levels"* [Video]. YouTube. https://youtu.be/EcinDlh82Ps?si=QQerPY6GScm95_jN.

[Accent's Way English with Hadar]. (2020, November 17). *"Tone of Voice: What You Really Mean"* [Video]. YouTube. https://youtu.be/hPQyHXc1ksA?si=Zfmt3IMtYh9dH4xS.

[Boys Town Press]. (2023, May 3). *"Appropriate Voice Tone"* [Video]. YouTube. https://www.youtube.com/watch?v=CWnKbVneh6I.

[Charisma on Command]. (2017, August 14). *"A Simple Game to Never Run Out of Things to Say in Conversation"* [Video]. YouTube. https://www.youtube.com/watch?v=QXiAPiw7vfc.

[Diana Jamison]. (2021, April 20). *"Social Emotional Learning Skill 10 Ignoring Distractions"* [Video]. YouTube. https://youtu.be/tuOeukujWWY?si=p4FHWWnFJbawc-5D.

[Ella Justice]. (2017, September 11). *"Power of Positive Words"* [Video]. YouTube. https://www.youtube.com/watch?v=I87tt00sMkM.

[Emily Atkins]. (2020, October 23). *"Disagreeing Respectfully"* [Video]. YouTube. https://www.youtube.com/watch?v=dVIqIyjOl20.

[English Singsing]. (2019, January 8). *"Asking for Permission: Role-Play Conversation for Kids"* [Video]. YouTube. https://www.youtube.com/watch?v=FZBjuwqn4xo&list=PLii5rkhsE0LfAiRdCqhWO17bq-2LIWKVU&index=5.

[Fact and Figures]. (2017, January 24). *"How to Give and Receive a Compliment"* [Video]. YouTube. https://www.youtube.com/watch?v=Fne1gW4nQSs.

[Hans Hiemenz]. (2020, September 9). *"Accepting 'No' as an Answer"* [Video]. YouTube. https://www.youtube.com/watch?v=Tt0LTY_nVCk.

[Hans Hiemenz]. (2020, November 15). *"Accepting Compliments"* [Video]. YouTube.
https://www.youtube.com/watch?v=89AfjKXpkkU.

[Hans Hiemenz]. (2022, February 11). *"Choosing Appropriate Words"* [Video].
YouTube. https://www.youtube.com/watch?v=u-s9-hN4Hns.

[Hans Hiemenz]. (2022, March 21). *"Making Positive Self Statements"* [Video]. YouTube.
https://www.youtube.com/watch?v=tMoHBVOM6Ks.

[Imaginary Pages]. (2023, May 4). *"Just Help by Sonia Sotomayor Read Aloud"* [Video].
YouTube. https://www.youtube.com/watch?v=5Pd-8-61Le4.

[Jessica Diaz]. (2019, December 4). *"Consequences for Kids: Character Education"* [Video].
YouTube. https://www.youtube.com/watch?v=LLZZYf_mlOA.

[Julie Bello The Innovative School Counselor]. (2017, October 22). *"Social Skill Making an Apology"* [Video].
YouTube. https://www.youtube.com/watch?v=I3C5S-gMSaQ.

[Kids Want to Know]. (2017, March 12). *"Why Do We Lose Control of Our Emotions?"* [Video]. YouTube.
https://www.youtube.com/watch?v=3bKuoH8CkFc.

[Loren Yost]. (2020, April 27). *"Read Aloud – A Little Respectful Spot: A Story about Respecting
People, Places, and Things"* [Video]. YouTube. https://www.youtube.com/watch?v=FjxKYNpdfjQ.

[Lovely Advice & Motivation]. (2017, January 25). *"5 Ways to Respectfully Disagree – How to Disagree Politely"*
[Video]. YouTube. https://www.youtube.com/watch?v=Y6EPw2FOEZA.

[Lynn Leinhos]. (2019, November 19). *"Story Time with Lynn: A Little Peaceful Spot by Diane Alber"* [Video].
YouTube. https://www.youtube.com/watch?v=0hnRCjjyhyo.

[Marvin Lee]. (2014, October 31). *"Getting the Teacher's Attention by Mrs. Lower's Class"* [Video].
YouTube. https://youtube.com/watch?v=wbrUHLIyBXc.

[Matthew Lambert]. (2019, August 12). *"Getting Another Person's Attention"* [Video].
YouTube. https://www.youtube.com/watch?v=XkQcMSdcOv8.

[Meghan Zigmond]. (2015, May 14). *"The Way You Say Your Words Matter"* [Video].
YouTube. https://youtu.be/rdPPnaGDxrs?si=XtJb-yY9s96krs8e.

[Mindful Schools]. (2015, January 26). *"Just Breathe"* [Video].
YouTube. https://www.youtube.com/watch?v=RVA2N6tX2cg.

[MX Kinder]. (2020, May 28). *"Toolbox: Apology and Forgiveness"* [Video].
YouTube. https://www.youtube.com/watch?v=tTifJOPCz7k.

[Participant]. (2013, November 22). *"Kid President's 20 Things We Should Say More Often"* [Video].
YouTube. https://www.youtube.com/watch?v=m5yCOSHeYn4.

[Patrick Haugens]. (2022, April 3). *"Zack Apologies"* [Video].
YouTube. https://www.youtube.com/watch?v=NvFWxNiLtZE.

[Reading Time with CJ]. (2021, May 1). *"Kids Book Read Aloud: Sorry, I Forgot to Ask!"* [Video].
YouTube. https://www.youtube.com/watch?v=4XRQ72WMNks.

[RHS PBL Team]. (2017, April 2). *"Kid President How to Disagree"* [Video]. YouTube. https://www.youtube.com/watch?v=dG5fkAgJmqc.

[RocketKids]. (2019, March 19). *"Stop Making Excuses & Own Your Actions"* [Video]. YouTube. https://www.youtube.com/watch?v=RGJpO2qHUbQ.

[SBCUSD]. (2019, October 11). *"Calm Down Centers: Creating a Safe Classroom Environment for Your Students"* [Video]. YouTube. https://www.youtube.com/watch?v=DQbuu5ufHyA.

[TDSocialSkills]. (2012, March 11). *"Social Skills Training: Taking Turns Speaking"* [Video]. YouTube. https://www.youtube.com/watch?v=3RjRZ9jMfs0.

[TED-Ed]. (2016, February 22). *"How Miscommunication Happens (and How to Avoid It) – Katherine Hampsten"* [Video]. YouTube. https://www.youtube.com/watch?v=gCfzeONu3Mo.

[TEDx Talks]. (2017, October 30). *"We Are All Different – and THAT'S AWESOME!"* [Video]. YouTube. https://www.youtube.com/watch?v=sQuM5e0QGLg.

[The Jesse Lewis Choose Love Movement]. (2016, October 1). *"What Is Forgiveness? Written and Voiced by Stephanie Bierman, Program Director"* [Video]. YouTube. https://www.youtube.com/watch?v=FFuHL6Izk6E.

[The Juicebox Jukebox]. (2018, November 13). *"Thankful by the Juicebox Jukebox/2021 Gratitude Appreciation Kids Songs Music Thanksgiving"* [Video]. YouTube. https://www.youtube.com/watch?v=YeSdQmO51Ps&t=7s.

[TPK Learning]. (2018, September 18). *"K12 Grade 2 – English: Introducing Yourself"* [Video]. YouTube. https://www.youtube.com/watch?app=desktop&v=dTaz4vnUk3s.

Acknowledgments

We extend a special "Thank You" to the many individuals whose insights and guidance helped us refine the curriculum and make the weekly lessons convenient and practical for educators and empowering and engaging for students. We appreciate all of their editorial support and feedback: Denise Pratt, Jennifer Buth-Bell, Lynette Zurek, Madelyn Dooley, Tara Eckstaine, Melanie Nuffer, Melissa Vidal, and Anne Hughes.

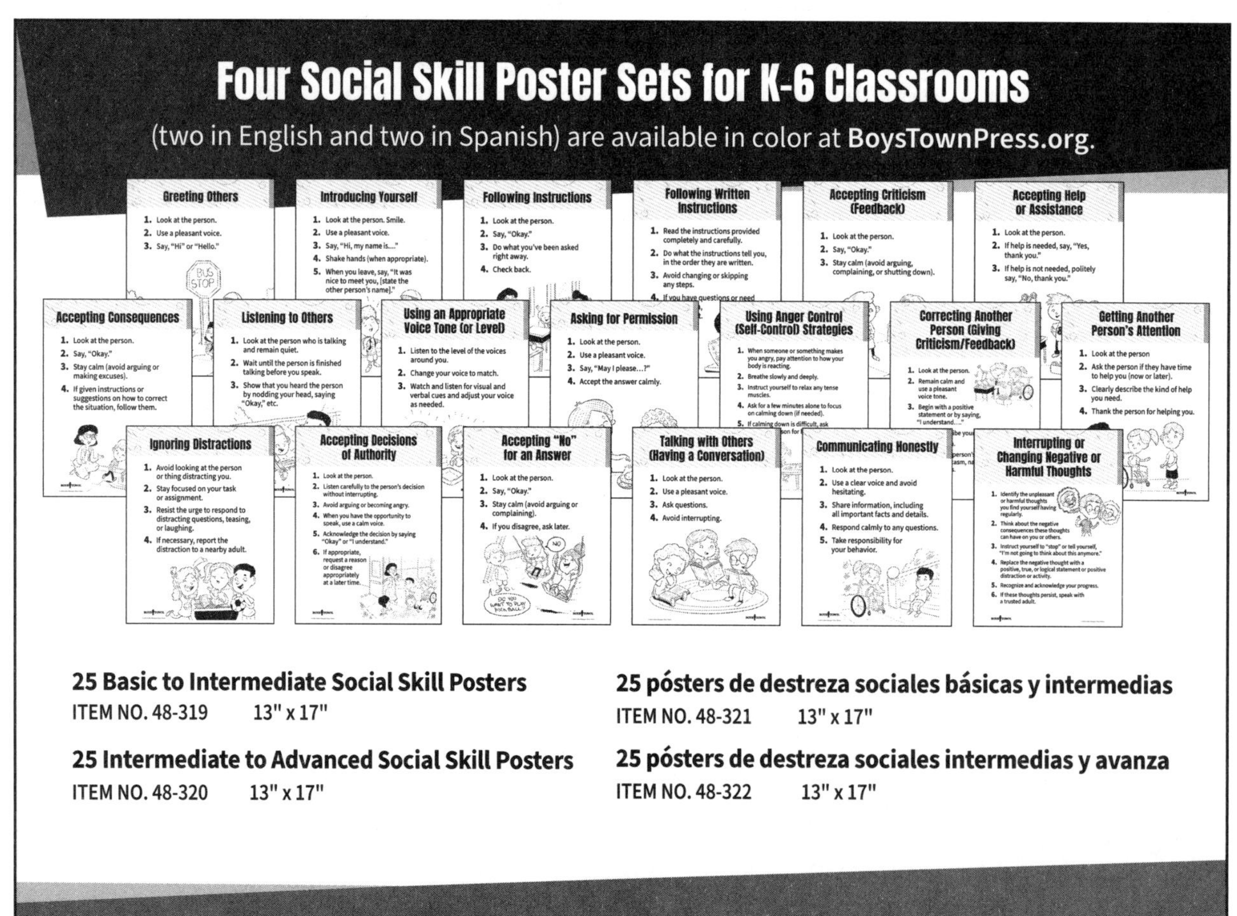

Award-Winning Titles from Julia Cook

Reinforce the social skills RJ learns in each book by ordering its corresponding teacher's activity guide and skill posters.

978-1-934490-20-4
978-1-934490-34-1 (SPANISH)
978-1-934490-23-5 (ACTIVITY GUIDE)

978-1-934490-25-9
978-1-934490-53-2 (SPANISH)
978-1-934490-27-3 (ACTIVITY GUIDE)

978-1-934490-28-0
978-1-934490-32-7 (ACTIVITY GUIDE)

978-1-934490-35-8
978-1-934490-37-2 (ACTIVITY GUIDE)

978-1-934490-43-3
978-1-934490-45-7 (ACTIVITY GUIDE)

978-1-934490-49-5
978-1-934490-51-8 (ACTIVITY GUIDE)

978-1-934490-67-9
978-1-934490-69-3 (ACTIVITY GUIDE)

Help kids get along.

Building RELATIONSHIPS

Help kids master the art of communicating.

COMMUNICATE with Confidence

Help kids take responsibility for their behavior.

Responsible ME!

978-1-944882-56-3

978-1-944882-24-2

OTHER TITLES: I Want to Be the Only Dog; Tease Monster; Hygiene... You Stink!; Making Friends Is an Art!; Cliques Just Don't Make Cents; Peer Pressure Gauge

978-1-944882-13-6

979-8-88907-000-9

OTHER TITLES: Gas Happens; Well, I Can Top That!

978-1-934490-90-7

978-1-934490-98-3

OTHER TITLES: Cheaters Never Prosper; But It's Not My Fault; The Procrastinator; What's In It For Me?

A book series that teaches children how to use collaboration, creativity, and compromise to influence others.

*It's My Way or the Highway
The Great Compromise
The "I" in Integrity
Good Things Come to Those Who Wait*

A book series celebrating unique kids who need support tackling shyness, following instructions, bedtime routines, and more!

*Herman Jiggle, Say Hello!
Herman Jiggle, Go to Sleep!*

*Herman Jiggle, It's Recess, not Restress!
Herman Jiggle, Just Be You!*

This series empowers kids with the skills and grit to grow their patience muscles, use flexible thinking, and become their best selves!

*Awesome Dawson Has Big Emotions
Awesome Dawson It's NOT Your Turn!*

For information on Boys Town and its Education Model, Common Sense Parenting®, and training programs:
LiftwithBoysTown.org | Parenting.org | training@boystown.org | 800-545-5771

Among our best sellers!
Bryan Smith's *Executive FUNction* Book Series

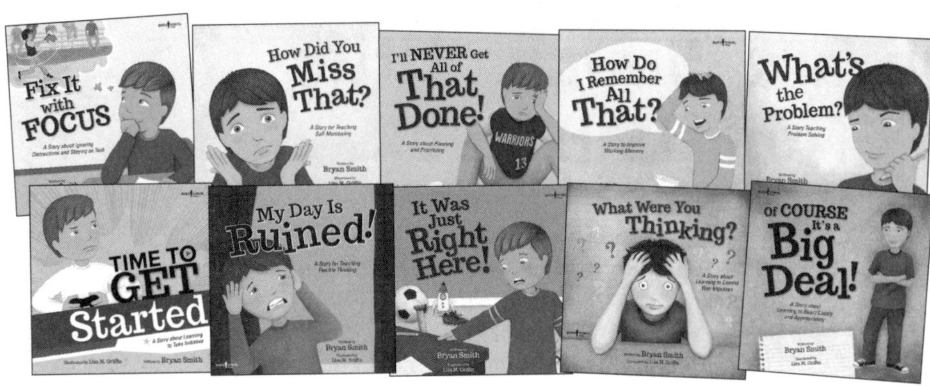

Stories that teach children how to plan, organize, manage time, and maintain self-control!

Jennifer Licate
GRADES 4-8

*A book series and accompanying activity guides focused on changing friendships,
finding your place, advocating for yourself, and being true to who you are.*

Steps to 196 Social Skills and More!

Teaching Social Skills to Youth, 4th Edition
An Easy-to-Follow Guide Teaching 196 Basic to Complex Life Skills

This definitive guide to social skills instruction now features thirteen new skills and their behavioral steps, fresh insights into providing culturally responsive treatment that respects individual identity, more inclusive language, and updated research on social-emotional learning and executive function. The 196 social and life skills will empower young people to have greater success in school, at home, on the job, and in their relationships.

Teaching Social Skills to Youth, 4th Edition
Jeff Tierney, M. Ed., Erin D. Green, M.S., with contributing author Kat McGrady, Ed.D., LCPC, NCC
ISBN: 978-1-944882-97-6

For parenting and educational books and other resources:
BoysTownPress.org | btpress@boystown.org | 800-282-6657